BE

AMAZED

BE

AMAZED

RESTORING AN ATTITUDE OF WONDER AND WORSHIP

OT COMMENTARY

MINOR PROPHETS

Warren W. Wiersbe

David C Cook®

transforming lives together

BE AMAZED
Published by David C. Cook
4050 Lee Vance View
Colorado Springs, CO 80918 U.S.A.

David C. Cook Distribution Canada
55 Woodslee Avenue, Paris, Ontario, Canada N3L 3E5

David C. Cook U.K., Kingsway Communications
Eastbourne, East Sussex BN23 6NT, England

David C. Cook and the graphic circle C logo
are registered trademarks of Cook Communications Ministries.

Unless otherwise noted, all Scripture quotations are taken from the King James Version
of the Bible. (Public Domain.) Scripture quotations marked NASB are taken from the
New American Standard Bible, © Copyright 1960, 1995 by The Lockman Foundation.
Used by permission; NIV are taken from the *Holy Bible, New International Version®.*
NIV®. Copyright © 1973, 1978, 1984 International Bible Society. Used by permission
of Zondervan. All rights reserved; NKJV are taken from the New King James Version.
Copyright © 1982 by Thomas Nelson, Inc. Used by permission. All rights reserved;
TLB are taken from *The Living Bible,* © 1971, Tyndale House Publishers, Wheaton,
IL 60189. Used by permission; and NRSV are taken from the New Revised Standard
Version Bible, copyright 1989, Division of Christian Education of the National Council
of the Churches of Christ in the United States of America. Used by permission. All
rights reserved. The author has added italics to Scripture quotations for emphasis.

LCCN 2010923217
ISBN 978-1-4347-6505-5
eISBN 978-0-7814-0442-6

© 1996 Warren W. Wiersbe

First edition of *Be Amazed* published by Victor Books® in 1996
© Warren W. Wiersbe, ISBN 978-1-56476-541-3

The Team: Karen Lee-Thorp, Amy Kiechlin, Sarah Schultz, Jack Campbell, and Karen Athen
Series Cover Design: John Hamilton Design
Cover Photo: Veer

Printed in the United States of America
Second Edition 2010

2 3 4 5 6 7 8 9 10

101310

CONTENTS

THE BIG IDEA

An Introduction to *Be Amazed*
by Ken Baugh

Not long ago I decided to do something that has been haunting me for years. I digitized twenty-one years of home movies. If you're a non-techie, what that means is that I copied a ton of home movies into my computer. I'm not done yet, but I've made a significant dent in the huge box of videos. And as I was importing each video into my computer, I watched the last twenty-one years of my life flash by. I cried as I watched both of my girls take their first steps, I laughed out loud as I watched clips from family vacations, fun times at Disneyland, the beach, first dance jitters, and the thrill of victory and the agony of defeat during countless dance recitals and sporting events. Right before my eyes, my two little girls grew from babies into beautiful, godly young women. I was also struck by the love I have for my wife and the incredible marriage we have shared over the years. And I noticed that I used to be a pretty handsome guy with a ripped stomach and a full head of hair—oh well, some things are bound to change.

You probably have watched your own home movies and experienced similar emotions as you watched your life pass before you, but something else happened to me that I was not expecting. As I reviewed my life and that of my family, I was also reminded of the incredible faithfulness of God. There were some pretty difficult seasons over the last twenty-one years, and those were not captured on tape, yet as I watched the movies, I remembered. I remembered the long and trying years of seminary. I remembered the experience of a devastating layoff from a church position that I loved. I remembered the uncertainty of moving to Virginia from California as I accepted a new church position. And yet, as I look back on those difficult seasons many years later, I can clearly see the hand of God as He guided and provided for my family and me.

I've often heard it said that hindsight is 20/20, and I must say that I agree. Not all of those *why* questions I asked of God years ago have been answered, but in hindsight I have the evidence of God's presence. Throughout my personal history I can look back and see the fingerprints of God's character all over my life, and I am reminded yet again that history is actually His story, where we discover His character, His attributes, and the purpose of life. As I look back on my personal history, I see God's attributes of love, patience, mercy, and power, to name a few.

The twelve books we call the Minor Prophets (because of their length, not their importance) represent God's story spanning 450 years as He revealed Himself to His people and the world. The commentary you hold in your hand will introduce you to six of those twelve prophets. I believe the Big Idea that runs through these books is how God reveals Himself throughout history to His people and a watching world. Let me outline three of God's attributes that you will see over and over again through these six prophetic books.

Attribute 1: The Sovereignty of God. The sovereignty of God is a running theme throughout each of the Minor Prophets as God shows Himself to be in control of all things. The important thing to remember about God's sovereignty is that He allows all things to happen in accordance with His divine purposes. Because you and I are His children, everything that happens to us is not the result of random events that just happen—everything that happens is part of God's ultimate plan. Now, make no mistake, God is not the author of evil. But He does allow evil things to happen to His people and works them into His divine purposes. I have discovered in my life and in the lives of countless others to whom I have ministered that what I may call "bad" is a tool in God's hand that He uses for my good and His glory.

The apostle Paul reminds us, "And we know that in all things God works for the good of those who love him, who have been called according to his purpose" (Rom. 8:28 NIV). This is no glib cliché or pat answer to "Why do bad things happen to good people?" Instead, it is the truth of God's sovereign, omnipotent reign over my life and this world that allows Him to take any situation and use it for His glory.

Attribute 2: The Holiness of God. For God to be holy simply means that He is morally perfect in every way and as such cannot tolerate sin. To sin is to miss the mark of moral perfection. God cannot sin because He is perfectly holy, and "in him there is no darkness at all" (1 John 1:5 NIV). God is literally the definition of holiness. His holiness raises a significant problem for every human being, because we are all sinners and as such are separated from a holy and righteous God. Yet God enables every person to become holy in His sight through repentance and acceptance of Christ's sacrifice on the cross as the payment for sin.

Throughout the Minor Prophets you will hear the prophets urgently calling God's people to repent in light of looming judgment. As a holy God, He must judge sin. So He sends these prophets to His people to urge them to repent and trust in Him for salvation. As you study the writings of these prophets, look for this common theme of repentance, the solution that God offers.

Attribute 3: The Love of God. The very fact that God sends a prophet to His people to warn them of coming judgment is evidence that God is love. He is gracious and merciful, not wanting His people to perish. God is a loving heavenly Father, and He disciplines His children when they sin. This discipline at times seems harsh, but He uses it to bring us to repentance.

The writer of Hebrews reminds us, "Endure hardship as discipline; God is treating you as sons.… God disciplines us for our good, that we may share in his holiness" (Heb. 12:7, 10 NIV). Throughout the Minor Prophets, God shows love to His people by giving them a chance to repent and, when they don't, bringing judgment not to punish but to discipline them and lead them to repentance. As you study the writings of these prophets, look for the fingerprints of God's love through His judgment and discipline.

The Minor Prophets span 450 years of history: It's God's story as He reveals Himself both to His people and to a watching world. Look for His attributes as you study, and make note of how often you see His sovereignty, holiness, and love. Then look back over your own personal history and *Be Amazed* at how God has worked in your life as His beloved son or daughter.

***

Dr. Wiersbe's commentaries have been a source of guidance and strength to me over the many years that I have been a pastor. His unique style is not overly academic, but theologically sound. He explains the deep truths of Scripture in a way that everyone can understand and apply. Whether you're a Bible scholar or a brand-new believer in Christ, you will benefit, as I have, from Warren's insights. With your Bible in one hand and Dr. Wiersbe's commentary in the other, you will be able to accurately unpack the deep truths of God's Word and learn how to apply them to your life.

Drink deeply, my friend, of the truths of God's Word, for in them you will find Jesus Christ, and there is freedom, peace, assurance, and joy.

—Ken Baugh
Pastor of Coast Hills Community Church
Aliso Viejo, California

A Word from the Author

When you compare them with the books written by Isaiah, Jeremiah, and Ezekiel, the Minor Prophets are "minor" only in size. The messages the Minor Prophets wrote are of major importance. In fact, their messages ought to fill us with wonder.

We should be amazed as Hosea describes God's jealous love and Joel pictures God's glorious kingdom. Jonah and Nahum both deal with the wicked city of Nineveh and amaze us with God's gracious long-suffering. Habakkuk watches the enemy approaching and invites us to be amazed at God's righteous judgment. Malachi amazes us with his revelation of God's contemptuous people, weary of serving the Lord.

Too many sleepy saints have lost their sense of wonder. The Minor Prophets shout at us to awaken us and invite us to open our eyes and be amazed at what God is doing in this world.

In this volume, I cover only six of the twelve Minor Prophets. Subsequent volumes will deal with Amos, Obadiah, Micah, and Zephaniah (*Be Concerned*), and Haggai and Zechariah (*Be Heroic*). The latter book will also include Ezra.

The Lord Jesus admonishes us "to believe all that the prophets have spoken" (Luke 24:25), and that includes the Minor Prophets. May we be faithful to receive and believe their messages and to obey what God tells us to do.

—Warren W. Wiersbe

HOSEA IN HIS TIME

(1 Kings 12; 2 Chronicles 26—32)

After the death of King Solomon, his son Rehoboam pursued a course that divided the nation into two kingdoms. Rehoboam reigned over Judah, the southern kingdom, composed of Judah and Benjamin; and Jeroboam II[1] ruled over the remaining ten tribes that formed the northern kingdom of Israel, also called Ephraim.

Fearful that the people would go back to Jerusalem to worship, Jeroboam I put golden calves at Bethel and Dan, thus leading the ten tribes into idolatry. Along with idolatry came immorality, and soon the religion of Israel become an evil blend of Jewish ritual and pagan idolatry. The people loved it.

The prophets were God's spokesmen to call Israel and Judah back to the covenant God had made with them at Mt. Sinai. But the people refused to listen, and both kingdoms suffered for their disobedience. Israel became an Assyrian vassal in 733 BC and then was conquered by Assyria in 722 BC. The Babylonians invaded Judah in 606 BC and destroyed Jerusalem in 586 BC. Thousands of Jews died, and thousands more went into exile in Babylon.

Hosea ministered in the northern kingdom from about 760 to 720 BC. Israel was enjoying great prosperity, but Hosea could see that the nation was rotten to the core; for honest government, pure religion, godly homes, and personal integrity had vanished from the land. Judgment was inevitable. Hosea faithfully preached the Word, but the nation refused to repent and was finally swallowed up by Assyria.

A Suggested Outline of the Book of Hosea

Theme: Devotion to the Lord is like faithfulness in marriage. Idolatry is
    like adultery.
Key verse: Hosea 2:20

I. Israel's Unfaithfulness Described (Hosea 1—3)

   1. God is gracious (Hosea 1:1—2:1)

   2. God is holy (Hosea 2:2–13)

   3. God is love (Hosea 2:14—3:5)

II. Israel's Sins Denounced (Hosea 4—7)

   1. Ignorance (Hosea 4:1–11)

   2. Idolatry (Hosea 4:12—5:15)

   3. Insincerity (Hosea 6:1—7:16)

III. Israel's Judgment Determined (Hosea 8—10)

   1. The Assyrian invasion (Hosea 8)

   2. The nation scattered (Hosea 9)

   3. Reaping what they have sown (Hosea 10)

IV. Israel's Restoration Declared (Hosea 11—14)

   1. God's past mercies (Hosea 11)

   2. God's present disciplines (Hosea 12—13)

   3. God's future promises (Hosea 14)

Chapter One

YOU MARRIED
A WHAT?

(Hosea 1—3)

Prophets sometimes do strange things. For three years, Isaiah embarrassed people by walking the streets dressed like a prisoner of war. For several months, Jeremiah carried a yoke on his shoulders. The prophet Ezekiel acted like a little boy and "played war," and once he used a haircut as a theological object lesson. When his wife suddenly died, Ezekiel even turned that painful experience into a sermon.[1]

Why did these men do these peculiar things?

"These peculiar things" were really acts of mercy. The people of God had become deaf to God's voice and were no longer paying attention to His covenant. The Lord called His servants to do these strange things—these "action sermons"—in hopes that the people would wake up and listen to what they had to say. Only then could the nation escape divine discipline and judgment.

But no prophet preached a more painful "action sermon" than Hosea. He was instructed to marry a prostitute named Gomer, who subsequently bore him three children, and he wasn't even sure the last two children were fathered by him. Then Gomer left him for another man, and Hosea had the humiliating responsibility of buying back his own wife.

What was this all about? It was a vivid picture of what the people of Israel had done to their God by prostituting themselves to idols and committing "spiritual adultery." Since God's people today face the same temptation (James 4:4), we need to heed what Hosea wrote for his people. Each of the persons in this drama—Hosea, Gomer, and the three children—teach us important spiritual lessons about the God whom Israel was disobeying and grieving.

THE CHILDREN: GOD IS GRACIOUS (1:1—2:1)

The times (1:1). Hosea names four kings of Judah and only one king of Israel, Jeroboam II. The kings of Judah, of course, belonged to David's dynasty, the only dynasty the Lord accepted (1 Kings 11:36; 15:4). The kings of Israel were a wicked lot who followed the sins of Israel's first king, Jeroboam I, and refused to repent and turn to God (2 Kings 13:6).

After Jeroboam II died, his son Zechariah reigned only six months and was assassinated by his successor, Shallum, who himself was assassinated after reigning only one month. Menahem reigned for ten years; his son Pekahiah ruled two years before being killed by Pekah, who was able to keep the throne for twenty years. He was slain by Hoshea, who reigned for ten years, the last of the kings of Israel. During his evil reign, the nation was conquered by Assyria, the Jews intermingled with the foreigners the Assyrians brought into the land, and the result was a mixed race known as the Samaritans.

What a time to be serving the Lord! Murder, idolatry, and immorality were rampant in the land, and nobody seemed to be interested in hearing the Word of the Lord! On top of that, God told His prophet to get married and raise a family!

The marriage (1:2). Here we meet a bit of a problem because not every Bible student agrees on the kind of woman Hosea married. Hosea either married a pure woman who later became a prostitute, or he married a prostitute who bore him three children.[2]

In the Old Testament, prostitution is symbolic of idolatry and unfaithfulness to God (Jer. 2—3; Ezek. 16; 23). Since the Jews were idolatrous from the beginning (Josh. 24:2–3, 14), it seems likely that Gomer would have to be a prostitute when she married Hosea, for this would best symbolize Israel's relationship to the Lord. God called Israel in the idolatry; He "married" them at Mount Sinai when they accepted His covenant (Ex. 19—21); and then He grieved over them when they forsook Him for the false gods of the land of Canaan. Like Gomer, Israel began as an idolater, "married" Jehovah, and eventually returned to her idolatry.

If Hosea had married a pure woman who later became unfaithful, "wife of whoredoms" in 1:2 has to mean "a wife prone to harlotry who will commit it later" but this seems to be a strained reading of the verse.[3] But could God ask His faithful servant to marry a defiled woman? Why not? We might as well ask, "Could God permit Ezekiel's wife to die?" Though marrying a prostitute might not be the safest step to take, such marriages were forbidden only to priests (Lev. 21:7). Salmon married Rahab the harlot, who became the great-grandmother of King David and an ancestress of Jesus Christ (Matt. 1:4–5).

The names (1:3–9). As with Isaiah's two sons (Isa. 7:3; 8:3), and numerous other people in Scripture, Gomer's three children were given meaningful names selected by the Lord.

The first child, a son, was called Jezreel (Hos. 1:4–5), which means "God sows" or "God scatters." Jezreel was a city in the tribe of Isaachar, near Mount Gilboa, and is associated with the drastic judgment that Jehu executed on the family of Ahab (2 Kings 9—10; and see 1 Kings 21:21–24). So zealous was Jehu to purge the land of Ahab's evil descendants that he murdered far more people than the Lord commanded, including King Ahaziah of Judah and forty-two of his relatives (2 Kings 9:27—10:14).

Through the birth of Hosea's son, God announced that He would avenge the innocent blood shed by Jehu and put an end to Jehu's dynasty in Israel. This was fulfilled in 752 BC when Zechariah was assassinated, the great-great-grandson of Jehu and the last of his dynasty to reign. God also announced that the whole kingdom of Israel would come to an end with the defeat of her army, which occurred in 724 BC.

The second child was a daughter named Lo-ruhamah (Hos. 1:6–7), which means "unpitied" or "not loved." God had loved His people and proved it in many ways, but now He would withdraw that love and no longer show them mercy. The expression of God's love is certainly unconditional, but our enjoyment of that love is conditional and depends on our faith and obedience. (See Deut. 7:6–12; 2 Cor. 6:14—7:1.) God would allow the Assyrians to swallow up the northern kingdom, but He would protect the southern kingdom of Judah (Isa. 36—37; 2 Kings 19).

Lo-ammi (Hos. 1:8–9) was the third child, a son, and his name means "not My people." Not only would God remove His mercy from His people, but He would also renounce the covenant He had made with them. It was like a man divorcing his wife and turning his back on her, or like a father rejecting his own son (see Ex. 4:22; Hos. 11:1).

The new names (1:10—2:1). Here is where the grace of God comes in, for God will one day change these names.[4] "Not my people" will become "My people," and "unloved" will become "My loved one." These new names reflect the nation's new relationship to God, for all of them will be "the sons of the living God."[5] Judah and Israel will unite as one nation and will submit to God's ruler, and the centuries' old division will be healed.

Instead of "Jezreel" being a place of slaughter and judgment, it will be a place of sowing, where God will joyfully sow His people in their own land and cause them to prosper. Today, the Jews are sown throughout the Gentile world (Zech. 10:9), but one day God will plant them in their own land and restore to them their glory. As God promised to Abraham, Israel will become like the sand on the seashore (Gen. 22:17).

When will these gracious promises be fulfilled for the Jews? When they recognize their Messiah at His return, trust Him, and experience His cleansing (Zech. 12:10—13:1). Then they will enter into their kingdom, and the promises of the prophets will be fulfilled (Isa. 11—12; 32; 35; Jer. 30—31; Ezek. 37; Amos 9:11–15).

The three children teach us about the grace of God. Now we'll consider the lesson that Gomer teaches us.

GOMER: GOD IS HOLY (2:2–13)

Hosea is preeminently the prophet of love, but unlike some teachers today, he doesn't minimize the holiness of God. We're told that "God is love" (1 John 4:8, 16), but we're also reminded that "God is light, and in him is no darkness at all" (1:5). God's love is a holy love, not a sentimental feeling that condones sin and pampers sinners.

The prophet focuses on three particular sins: idolatry (spiritual adultery), ingratitude, and hypocrisy.

(1) Idolatry (vv. 2–5a). God speaks to the children and tells them to rebuke their mother for her unfaithfulness. Israel was guilty of worshipping the gods of the pagan nations around them, especially the Canaanite rain god, Baal. Whenever there was a drought or a famine in the land, the Jews repeatedly turned to Baal for help instead of turning to the Lord. (See 1 Kings 18—19.) Pagan worship involved sensual fertility rites; and for these rites, both male and female prostitutes were provided. In a literal as well as a symbolic sense, idolatry meant prostitution.[6]

Since the people were acting like prostitutes, God would treat them like prostitutes and shame them publicly. He would no longer claim the nation as His wife because she had broken the solemn marriage covenant and consorted with idols. According to Hebrew law, adultery was a capital crime, punishable by death, but God announced that He would discipline Israel and not destroy her.[7]

Unfaithfulness to the Lord is a serious sin, just as unfaithfulness to one's mate is a serious sin. The man who says he's 90 percent faithful to his wife isn't faithful at all. As Israel was tempted to forsake God for idols, the church is tempted to turn to the world system that hates God and wants nothing to do with God.

We must be careful not to love the world (1 John 2:15–17), be friendly with the world (James 4:4), become spotted by the world (1:27), or conform to the world (Rom. 12:2). Each believer and each local church must remain true to Jesus Christ the Bridegroom until He returns to take His bride to the heavenly wedding (2 Cor. 11:1–4; Eph. 5:22–33; Rev. 19:6–9).

(2) Ingratitude (vv. 5b–9). Instead of thanking the true God for His blessings of food, water, and clothing, the nation thanked the false gods and used those gifts to serve idols. What ingratitude! God provided rain for the land (Deut. 11:8–17), but the Israelites gave the credit to Baal, the rain god. Because it is God who gives us power to earn wealth (8:17–18) and enjoy the blessings of life (1 Tim. 6:17), we must thank Him and acknowledge His goodness. What wickedness it is to take the gifts of God and use them to worship false gods!

God had every right to abandon His people, but instead, He chose to discipline them. The nation would chase after false gods, but Jehovah would block their paths and confuse their plans so that they would stumble on the way. He would take back His gifts and leave the nation as naked as a newborn baby and as barren as a desert.

It's remarkable how many times God's people are admonished in Scripture to be thankful. I've noted at least fifteen places where we're commanded to "give thanks to the Lord," and Psalm 100:4 and Colossians 3:15 both admonish us to be thankful. Both Jesus and Paul set the example by giving thanks often to the Lord for His blessings. One of the first steps toward rebellion against God is a refusal to give God thanks for His mercies (Rom. 1:21). God will not allow us to enjoy His gifts and at the same time ignore the Giver, for this is the essence of idolatry.

(3) Hypocrisy (vv. 10–13). The people still enjoyed celebrating the

Hebrew festivals, but in their hearts, they gave the glory to Baal and the other false gods that they worshipped. Unfortunately, the same sin was being committed by their brothers and sisters in the temple of Jerusalem (Isa. 1). How easy it is to attend divine services and go through the motions of worshipping God when our hearts are really far from Him (Matt. 15:7–9).

But the truth would eventually come out, for God would judge His people and expose their hypocrisy. He would take away their blessings and abandon them to their sins, for one of the greatest judgments God can inflict on any people is to let them have their own way. God is holy and will not permit His people to enjoy sin for long or to live on substitutes. Eight times in the Bible we read, "Be holy, for I am holy"; God means what He says.

HOSEA: GOD IS LOVE (2:14—3:5)

The three children have taught us about the grace of God, and Gomer has taught us about the holiness of God. Now Hosea will teach us about the love of God.

"Hosea takes his place among the greatest lovers of all the ages," wrote Kyle M. Yates. "His love was so strong that the vilest behavior could not dull it. … Gomer broke his heart but she made it possible for him to give to the world a picture of the heart of the divine Lover."[8]

God's love promised (vv. 14–23). The repeated "I will" statements in these verses assure us that God has a wonderful future planned for the Jewish people. Let's note His promises.

He begins with *"I will allure"* (v. 14). God doesn't try to force His people to love him. Instead, He "allures" (woos) them as a lover woos his beloved, seeking her hand in marriage. Certainly God spoke tenderly to His people through His Word and through the manifold blessings He bestowed on them in their land. Just as He led her through the wilderness and "married" her at Sinai, so God will meet His beloved in the wilderness in the last days and lead her into her land and her glorious kingdom.

The next promise is *"I will give"* (v. 15) as the Lord guarantees a return to their land and a restoration of their prosperity. Once again, the Lord changes the meaning of a name, this time, "the Valley of Achor." To Israel, the Valley of Achor ("trouble") was the place where Achan stole from God and brought shameful defeat to Israel's army (Josh. 7), but that memory would be erased from their minds. The valley would become a "door of hope" through which Israel would enter into a new life. The experience would produce singing, as when Israel escaped from Egypt and saw her enemies defeated before their very eyes (Ex. 14–15). "And Sharon shall be a fold of flocks, and the valley of Achor a place for the herds to lie down in, for my people that have sought me" (Isa. 65:10). This is an Old Testament version of Romans 8:28, for only the Lord can take defeat and shame and turn it into victory and glory.

God's third promise is *"I will take away"* (Hos. 2:16–17). God declares an end to idolatry among His people. They would have a new vocabulary and the "baals" would never be named again. "Ishi" means "my husband" in Hebrew and "Baali" means "my master." Both terms were used by Jewish wives when addressing their husbands, but in the future kingdom, every Jew will call God "my Husband," for the divine marriage relationship will be restored. Israel will no longer prostitute herself before idols, but will love and serve the true living God.

God's fourth promise is *"I will betroth"* (vv. 18–20). God's wooing of Israel will result in her yielding to Him and entering into a covenant relationship that would never end. This new covenant will include a restored creation (see Gen. 9:1–10; Rom. 8:18–22) and peace among the nations. Among the "wedding gifts" will be such blessings as righteousness, justice, love, compassion, and faithfulness—everything that Israel had lacked during her years of separation from her Husband, Jehovah God.

The fifth promise is *"I will respond"* (Hos. 2:21–22 NIV), (KJV, "I will hear"). These two verses describe a tremendous cosmic conversation in which the Lord speaks to the heavens and the earth, and they respond to each other and bring blessings to God's people. The heavens send the rain, the earth brings forth the produce, and the Lord sends His rich blessings. It's the picture of a restored universe where sin and death no longer reign (Rom. 5:12–21).

The final promise in this text is *"I will plant"* (Hos. 2:23 NIV). The word *Jezreel* means "God sows." The image is that of God sowing His people in their land the way a farmer sows seed. He says to them, "You are my people." They respond, "You are my God" (NIV). This relates back to the names of the children that God in His grace had changed.

God's love pictured (3:1–5). This is another "action sermon" as Hosea reclaims his estranged wife and brings her home to himself. Gomer had left Hosea and was living with a lover, another picture of the way Israel had treated the Lord. Hosea had to buy her back at a cost of fifteen pieces of silver (half the price of a slave, Ex. 21:32) and about ten bushels of barley. This was not an exorbitant price, but she had cheapened herself by her sins. We need to remember that God has purchased us at the tremendous cost of the precious blood of His only Son (1 Peter 1:18–19).

Hosea 3:3 suggests that Hosea didn't immediately enter into intimate relations with Gomer, but waited awhile to make sure she would be true to him. It's also possible that he wanted to make sure she wasn't pregnant with another man's child. But even this has a spiritual message attached to it: Israel today, though purchased by their Messiah (John 11:47–52; Isa. 53:8), has not yet returned to the Lord.

Israel today is without a king because she rejected her King and therefore has no kingdom. "We will not have this man to reign over us" (Luke 19:14). "We have no king but Caesar" (John 19:15). She has no prince because there is no reigning dynasty in Israel. All the records were destroyed when the Romans captured Jerusalem in AD 70, and nobody can prove to which tribe he or she belongs.

The Israelites have no sacrifice because they have no temple, altar, or priesthood. They don't have a pillar (image) or a household god (teraphim), because idolatry was purged from their culture during the Babylonian captivity. (Like the Gentiles, they may have other kinds of idols in their hearts!) They lack an ephod (Ex. 28:1–14) because they have no high priest. The only High Priest God will acknowledge is the interceding Son of God in heaven.

But there is an "afterword"! Israel won't stay "without," for she will see her Messiah, repent of her sins, and say, "You are my God." They will enter into that blessed relationship in which the Lord says, "You are My people." This will occur in "the latter days" when the messianic King sits on David's throne and judges righteously (Matt. 19:28; Luke 1:32–33).

The key word is *return* (Hos. 3:5), a word that's used twenty-two times in Hosea's prophecy. When Israel repents and returns to the Lord, then the Lord will return to bless Israel (2:7–8). God has returned to His place and left Israel to herself (5:15) until she seeks Him and says, "Come, and let us return to the Lord" (6:1 NKJV).

This is Hosea's message: "O Israel, return to the LORD thy God…. Take with you words, and turn to the LORD: say unto him, Take away all iniquity, and receive us graciously" (14:1–2).

That prayer is good for any sinner, Jew or Gentile. To summarize:

God is gracious, and no matter what "name" our birth has given to us, He can change it and give us a new beginning. Even the "valley of trouble" can become a "door of hope."

God is holy, and He must deal with sin. The essence of idolatry is enjoying the gifts but not honoring the Giver. To live for the world is to break God's heart and commit "spiritual adultery."

God is love and promises to forgive and restore all who repent and return to Him. He promises to bless all who trust Him.

QUESTIONS FOR PERSONAL REFLECTION OR GROUP DISCUSSION

1. From what you know about the prophets as you begin this study, does being a prophet seem like a glamorous job to you? Explain.

2. Why do you think God often chose "action sermons," such as Hosea's marriage to Gomer, in order to deliver His messages through the prophets?

3. What might Hosea have been feeling or thinking through it all? What might Gomer's view of it have been?

4. In the examples of Gomer and Rahab, God shows His amazing love for sinners. How do the responses of Gomer and Rahab differ?

5. How did God continue His "action sermon" with Hosea and Gomer's children?

6. Who are some other biblical characters whose names were given or changed by God? Why did God do this?

7. God disciplines us "so that we may share His holiness" (Heb. 12:10 NASB). What were some aspects of God's discipline in Hosea's time? How does He discipline a contemporary believer in our country today?

8. Why might the refusal to give thanks be one of the first steps to rebellion? How does this compare with forgetting to give thanks?

9. If Hosea and Gomer were your neighbors, what advice would you give Hosea? How does "tough love" fit into this action sermon? What is the real point of the marriage of Hosea and Gomer?

10. What are the three attributes of God that Wiersbe highlights in this portion of Scripture? Which one of these do you need to grasp more fully? Why that particular one?

Chapter Two

WHAT WILL I
DO WITH YOU?

(Hosea 4—10)

I ndeed I tremble for my country when I reflect that God is just."

Thomas Jefferson wrote those words about the United States of America, and as the prophet Hosea surveyed the kingdom of Israel, he would have agreed. From his bitter experience with his wife, Hosea knew that sin not only breaks the heart of God, but also offends the holiness of God, for "righteousness and justice are the foundation of [His] throne" (Ps. 89:14 NKJV).

God wanted to forgive the sins of His people and restore their fellowship with Him, but they weren't ready. They not only would not repent, but they also wouldn't even admit that they had sinned! So God conducted a trial and brought them to the bar of justice. It's a basic spiritual principle that until people experience the guilt of conviction, they can't enjoy the glory of conversion.

GOD CONVENES THE COURT (4:1—5:15)

Just as Hosea had experienced a quarrel with his wife, so God had a quarrel with His estranged wife, the people of Israel. But it wasn't a personal quarrel; it was an official controversy: "The Lord has a charge to bring against you who live in the land" (Hos. 4:1 NIV). The picture of God bringing men and nations to trial in His courtroom is a familiar one in Scripture (see Isa. 1:12; Jer. 2:9, 29; 25:31; Mic. 6:2; Rom. 3:19). "Rise up, O Judge of the earth; pay back to the proud what they deserve" (Ps. 94:2 NIV).

The Judge read the charges to the accused as they stood before God.

The nation as a whole (4:1b–3). The basis for judgment was the holy law of God, the covenant God made with Israel at Mount Sinai. "All that the Lord hath spoken we will do," was their promise (Ex. 19:8), but that promise was soon broken. Just as Gomer didn't take her marriage vows seriously but went to live with another man, so Israel reneged on her promises to God and turned to pagan idols. There was no faithfulness (truth) in the land, no loyal love to the Lord.

When people reject God's covenant, they begin to exploit each other, for the Ten Commandments deal with our relationship with our neighbor as well as with the Lord. If we love the Lord, we will also love our neighbor (Matt. 22:34–40; Rom. 13:8–10). But there was no mercy in the land, no love for one's neighbor, no compassion for the poor and needy. People were falsehearted toward God and hardhearted toward one another.

The basic sin was ignorance; there was "no knowledge of God in the land." "My people are destroyed for lack of knowledge" (Hos. 4:6).[1] This means much more than knowledge about God; it refers to a personal knowledge of God. The Hebrew word describes a husband's most intimate relationship with his wife (Gen. 4:1; 19:8). To know God is to have a personal relationship with Him through faith in Jesus Christ (John 17:3).

The Judge pointed to the Ten Commandments (Ex. 20:1–17) and reminded the people of how they had violated His law by pronouncing curses, telling lies, murdering, stealing, and committing adultery. As a result, they had brought suffering to themselves, to the land, and even to the animals. God's covenant promise was that He would bless the land if the people obeyed Him, but that He would punish the land if they disobeyed (Lev. 26; Deut. 27—28).

The land belonged to God (Lev. 25:23), and the sins of the people polluted the land (18:25–28; 26:32–33). Natural calamities like droughts, famines, and the devastations of war were sometimes sent by God to discipline His people. Whether to bless or to judge, God always keeps His covenant promises.[2]

The priests (4:4–14). When Jeroboam I set up his own religious system in Israel, many of the true priests fled to Judah; so the king ordained priests of his own choosing (2 Chron. 11:13–15). Of course, these counterfeit priests knew neither the Lord nor His law. They were primarily interested in having an easy job that would provide them with food, clothing, and pleasure, especially opportunities to be with the shrine prostitutes. "Don't blame the people for what's happening," Hosea said to the corrupt priests, "because they're only following your bad example!"

When you obey God's Word, you walk in the light and don't stumble (Prov. 3:21–26; 4:14–19), but when you reject the Word, you walk in the darkness and can't find your way (Isa. 8:20). Worldly and ignorant spiritual leaders produce worldly and ignorant people, and this brings destruction to the land. The phrase "your mother" in Hosea 4:5 (NIV) refers to the nation of Israel (2:2, 5). As goes spiritual leadership, so goes the church; as goes the church, so goes morality; and as goes morality, so goes the nation. God's people are both salt and light in society (Matt. 5:13–16); when they are corrupt, society becomes corrupt.

God rejected Jeroboam's man-made religion[3] and warned the priests that their easy jobs would soon end in disaster. Instead of seeking God's will, they consulted their idols.[4] The more the people sinned, the more food the priests enjoyed. The more shrines the people built, the more they and the priests could indulge in lustful pleasures as they participated in the fertility rites. But the rites wouldn't accomplish anything, because

God would cause the population and the produce to decrease instead of increase. Furthermore, the priests' own daughters and daughters-in-law would become shrine prostitutes and commit adultery![5] Their sins would bring judgment to their families and to the land.

The spectators in the court (4:15–19). Now the prophet turns to the people of the southern kingdom of Judah who were carefully watching events in Israel. Hosea's warning is clear: Don't meddle in the affairs of Israel because their doom is sure! "Ephraim is joined to idols: let him alone" (v. 17). The people of Judah were supposed to worship in Jerusalem and not go to the hill shrines in Israel or to the special shrines at Gilgal[6] and Bethel. (Hosea calls Bethel "Bethaven," which means "house of evil or deceit." Bethel means "house of God.") Israel was like a stubborn heifer, not a submissive lamb; and God's whirlwind of judgment would sweep the kingdom away.

Priests, rulers, and people (5:1–7). This is a summation of the evidence that the Judge applied to all the accused. He condemned the leaders for trapping innocent people and exploiting them. There was no justice in the land. They were sinking deep in sin and lacked the power to repent and turn back to God, for their sins had paralyzed them.

What was the cause? They did not know the Lord (5:4; 6:3) and their arrogance only led them to stumble and fall (5:5; Prov. 16:18). Even if they came to the Lord with entire flocks and herds to sacrifice, God would not meet them; for He had withdrawn Himself from them. He rejected their illegitimate children,[7] and their monthly feasts would soon become funerals.

The sentence is pronounced (5:8–15). There could be only one verdict: "Guilty!" A day of judgment was coming when the cites of Israel would be conquered by the invading Assyrian army and the citizens taken into captivity. "Ephraim will be laid waste on the day of reckoning" (5:9 NIV).[8] The inner decay of the nation was like the slow hidden destruction caused by a moth (v. 12), but the coming of the Assyrians was like the sudden open attack of a lion (v. 14). Both were unavoidable and both brought ruin.

Israel and Judah were weak, sick nations (Isa. 1:5–6; Jer. 30:12–13), but instead of turning to the Lord for healing, both of them turned to the king of Assyria for help (Hos. 5:13).[9] They needed prayer and true repentance, but instead, they trusted politics and useless treaties. All the Lord could do was withdraw and wait for them to seek His face in truth and humility.

GOD REJECTS THE APPEAL (6:1—7:16)

It isn't unusual for the accused in a trial to express regret and remorse for what they've done and to ask for another chance. That's just what Israel did, but God anticipated their hypocritical subterfuge and exposed not only their duplicity but also the sinful way they had treated their Lord.

The nation's false repentance (6:1–3). When you read these words, you get the impression that the nation is sincerely repenting and seeking the Lord, but when you read what God says, you see how shallow their "confession" really was. "They do not return to the Lord their God, nor seek him" (7:10). "They have spoken lies against me" (v. 13). "They return, but not to the most High" (v. 16). What went wrong with this "confession"?

To begin with, their concern was for healing and not for cleansing. They saw their nation in difficulty and wanted God to "make things right," but they did not come with broken hearts and surrendered wills. They wanted happiness, not holiness, a change of circumstances, but not a change in character. Many times in my own ministry I've met people in trouble who treated God like a celestial lifeguard who should rescue them from danger but not deliver them from their sins. They shed tears of remorse over their suffering, but not tears of repentance over their sin.

Furthermore, the people of Israel thought that the remedy would work quickly: "After two days will he revive us; in the third day he will raise us up" (6:2). What blind optimism! They were like the false prophets in Jeremiah's day who offered the nation superficial remedies but never got to the heart of the problem (Jer. 6:14; 8:11–16). They were like physicians putting suntan lotion on a cancerous tumor instead of calling for drastic surgery. Expecting a "quick fix" is one of the marks of an unrepentant heart that doesn't want to pay the price for deep cleansing (Ps. 51:6–7).

There is a third evidence of their shallowness: They saw forgiveness and restoration as a "mechanical" thing that was guaranteed and not as a relational matter that involved getting right with God. To paraphrase Hosea 6:3, "If we seek Him, His blessing is sure to come just as the dawn comes each morning and the rains come each spring and winter." This is formula religion, like getting a candy bar out of a vending machine: put in the money, push the button, and out comes the candy. The Christian life is a relationship with God, and relationships aren't based on cut-and-dried formulas.

One more evidence of their shallowness is the fact that they depended on religious words rather than righteous deeds. When we truly repent, our words will come from broken hearts and they will cost us something. Hosea considered words to be like "spiritual sacrifices" brought to the Lord (14:2), and we must not give Him something cheap (2 Sam. 24:24). Words can reveal or conceal, depending on the honesty and humility of the sinner.[10] We must take to heart the warning in Ecclesiastes 5:1–2.

The nation's true condition (6:4—7:16). In a series of vivid similes and metaphors, Hosea revealed the true character of the people of Israel.

Their love for the Lord was like a morning cloud and the dew (6:4–11). Early in the morning, the dew looks like sparkling jewels, but as soon as the sun comes up, the dew is gone. Israel's devotion to the Lord was temporary, lovely but not lasting. To give some substance to their faith, God sent them His prophets with the Word of God, which is like a penetrating sword (Eph. 6:17) and a flash of lightning (Hos. 6:5 NIV), but the people turned a deaf ear.

God doesn't want our relationship with Him to be one of shallow, transient feelings and empty words and rituals, hearts that are enthusiastic one day and frigid the next. "For I desired mercy [loyal love], and not sacrifice, and the knowledge of God more than burnt offerings" (Hos. 6:6). A superficial ritual can never take the place of sincere love and faithful obedience (1 Sam. 15:22–23; Amos 5:21–24; Mic. 6:6–8; Matt 9:13; 12:7).

"But like Adam they have transgressed the covenant" (Hos. 6:7 NASB).[11] God promised Adam His blessings if he obeyed His commands, but Adam deliberately destroyed and plunged the human race into sin and death (Rom. 5:12–21; 1 Cor. 15:21–22). God promised Israel the blessings of the Promised Land if they would obey Him (Deut. 28), but they broke the covenant and suffered the consequences. For both Israel and Judah, God had appointed a harvest, and they would reap just what they had sown (Gal. 6:7–8).

Their lust was like an overheated oven (Hos. 7:1–7). It's probable that the last statement in 6:11 should be joined with 7:1 to read, "When I [would have] returned the captivity of my people, when I would have healed Israel." What prevented God from helping His distressed people? They wanted Him to act on their terms and not according to the condition of His holy covenant. They thought they could get away with their many sins, but God saw them all and remembered them (v. 2; contrast Heb. 10:16–17).

Their passion for sin was like a fire in an oven: Bank the fire at night, and it will be ready to blaze out in the morning. The oven was so hot that the baker could ignore it all night and know it would be ready for baking his bread in the morning. The "fuel" for the fire was wine, for alcohol and sin often go together.

Hosea describes a palace celebration during which the king and his officers get drunk, and this gives the king's enemies opportunity to overthrow him and even kill him. Remember, Israel had five kings in thirteen years, and four kings were assassinated in twenty years. From Jeroboam I, the first king of Israel, to Hoshea, the last king, there were nine different dynasties! Because the leaders were far from the Lord, the political situation was confused and corrupt.

The third simile is that of a half-baked cake (Hos. 7:8). The nomadic peoples of the East baked their bread on hot rocks. If the dough wasn't turned, one side of the loaf would be burned and the other side uncooked. Instead of remaining separate from the nations, Israel mixed with the nations and became like them. Because of her compromising political posture, the nation was "burned" by Assyria on one side and left uncooked on the other.

When it comes to our relationship with the Lord, we must be thorough and not "half-baked." His gracious work must permeate our whole being so that heart, mind, and strength are all devoted to Him. Compromise with the world leads to unbalanced conduct and immature character.

Continuing the theme of compromise, Hosea pictures Israel as a man getting gray and not knowing it (vv. 9–10). By mixing with the nations and ignoring the Lord, the nation was secretly losing her strength, like someone getting older and weaker but in her pride refusing to admit it. This is the tragedy of undetected losses that quietly led to ultimate failures. Samson made this mistake (Judg. 16:20) and so did the church in Laodicea (Rev. 3:17). Israel saw her political strategy failing, but the leaders still refused to turn to the Lord. "The pride of Israel" (Hos. 7:10; see 5:5) refers to Israel's national glory, which had greatly eroded since the days of David and Solomon. Selfish politicians and corrupt priests had brought the nation to ruin.

In their political policies, the Israelites were like a "silly dove" (7:11–12). First they turned to Egypt for help and then to Assyria, and both nations proved to be false allies (5:13; 8:8–10; 12:1). If the leaders had listened to the prophets, they would have known that Assyria would one day invade the land (9:3; 10:5–6; Isa. 7:18—8:10). God warned that Israel's "flying here and there" would come to an end when He caught them in His net and gave them to the king of Assyria. God is in control of the nations, but His people would not obey Him.

According to the covenant God had with His people, the Jews could trade with the other nations, but they were not to enter into political alliances that would compromise their obedience to the Lord. "I see a people who live apart and do not consider themselves one of the nations" (Num. 23:9 NIV). "You are to be holy to me because I, the Lord, am holy, and I have set you apart from the nations to be my own" (Lev. 20:26 NIV). Solomon used many wives to form alliances with other nations, and this was the beginning of the nation's downfall (1 Kings 11:1ff.).

The final image is a "faulty bow" (Hos. 7:13–16 NIV), because God couldn't depend on Israel to be faithful. (This image is also used in Ps. 78:57.) God had called Israel and trained them, so they should have been able to "hit the target." But because they had strayed from the Lord, rebelled against Him, lied to Him (in their feigned repentance), and refused to call upon Him, they could not win the battle.

As we review these images, we might take inventory of our own devotion to the Lord. How lasting is it? How deep is it? How strong is it? How serious is it? How dependable is it?

GOD PRONOUNCES THE SENTENCE (8:1—10:15)

For the second time, Hosea calls for the trumpet to be blown (8:1; 5:8). According to Numbers 10, the Jews used trumpets to announce special occasions, to sound alarms, to gather the people for assemblies, and to proclaim war. This call was a trumpet of alarm because the enemy was coming and God was giving His people opportunity to repent. Hosea again used a number of familiar images to show the people what God would do to them because of their sin.

The eagle (8:1–6). "The house of the Lord" refers to the nation of Israel, for the people were God's dwelling place (Hos. 9:15; Ex. 15:17; Num. 12:7). The Assyrian eagle was about to swoop down and destroy God's house because the nation was given over to idolatry, and the leaders were not seeking God's will in their decisions. They made kings and removed kings to satisfy their own desires, and they manufactured gods (especially the golden calves at Bethel and Dan) that could not help them.[12]

Sowing and reaping (8:7). The concept of sowing and reaping as it relates to conduct is often used in Scripture (Job 4:8; Prov. 22:8; Jer. 12:13; Gal. 6:7–8), and Hosea used it twice (Hos. 8:7; 10:12–13). In their idolatry and political alliances, the Israelites were trying to sow seeds that would produce a good harvest, but they were only sowing the wind—vanity, nothing—and would reap the whirlwind. Nothing could stop the force of the Assyrian army. The harvest would be more powerful than the seed!

The sowing/reaping image continues with the picture of a blighted crop of grain. The rulers of Israel thought their worship of Baal and their foreign alliances would produce a good crop of peace and prosperity; but when the time came for the harvest, there was nothing to reap. And even where heads of grain did appear, the enemy reaped the harvest and Israel gained nothing. In the image of the wind, Hosea said, "You will reap far more than you sowed, and it will be destructive!" In the image of the grain, he said, "You will reap nothing at all, and your enemies will get the benefit of all the promises you made."

Worthless pottery (8:8). There was no grain for Israel to swallow, but she herself would be "swallowed up" by Assyria. She was a useless vessel "in which no one delights" (NASB). Their compromise had so cheapened them that Israel was of no value to the community of nations. Nobody feared them, nobody courted them, nobody wanted them.

A stupid donkey (Hos. 8:9a). Israel wanted to be a part of the alliances that were forming to fight Assyria, but she was actually very much alone.

She was like a dumb animal that had lost its way in the wilderness. Israel had forsaken her God, and she had been forsaken by her allies, so she was abandoned to face a terrible future alone.

A prostitute (8:9b–10). In negotiating with the Gentile nations for protection, Ephraim (Israel) acted like a common prostitute selling herself for money. Israel's kings paid tribute to the king of Assyria and also sent gifts to Egypt (12:1). Instead of being faithful to her Husband, Jehovah God, Israel prostituted herself to the Gentile nations—and lost everything. God promised to gather them together for judgment, and they would "waste away" (NIV) under the ruthless hand of the Assyrian king.

Egyptian bondage (8:11—9:9). Hosea mentions Egypt thirteen times in his book, and these references fall into three distinct categories: past—the exodus of the Jews from Egypt (2:15; 11:1; 12:9, 13; 13:4); present—Israel's unholy alliances with Egypt (7:11, 16; 12:1); future—Egypt as a symbol of their impending bondage to Assyria (8:13; 9:3, 6; 11:5, 11). Three times in this section, the prophet announces, "They shall return to Egypt" (8:13; 9:3, 6); but 11:5 makes it clear that "Egypt" is a symbol for Assyrian bondage: "He shall not return to the land of Egypt; but the Assyrian shall be his king" (NKJV).

The prophet contrasts the past exodus from the bondage of Egypt with the impending "exodus" into the bondage of Assyria, the new "Egypt." When the Jews left Egypt, they had not yet received the law, nor did they have the tabernacle and its system of sacrifices. But now the Jews had heard the law for centuries, and the temple had been standing since Solomon's time. Yet they ignored the law, and the priesthood became corrupt. The NIV catches the irony in 8:11, "Though Ephraim built many altars for sin offerings, these have become altars for sinning."

Instead of trusting the Lord to protect her from Assyria, Israel fortified her towns and sought help from foreign nations, and from a spiritual point of view, this was like prostitution. (During the harvest season, prostitutes

frequented the threshing floors where the men slept to guard the grain.)
The harvest season was a time of great joy (Isa. 9:3), but there would be no
joy in Israel. And when the people ended up in a foreign land, everything
would be unclean to them, but they were an unclean people anyway, so
what difference would it make?

Agriculture (9:10—10:10). God reviews the history of His relationship
with the Jews. You don't find grapes in the desert, but if you did, it would
thrill you. That's how God felt when He called Israel. The early fruit of
the fig tree is especially good, and Israel was special to the Lord. But this
joyful experience didn't last, for King Balak gave Israel her first taste of
Baal worship, and the nation indulged in idolatry and immorality with its
neighbors (Num. 25).

God planted His people in a special land, but they polluted the land
with their idols (Hos. 9:13). The more prosperous they became, the more
they turned away from God. Now they must suffer a bitter harvest for
their sins, they and their children.[13] The nation is blighted, having no
roots and bearing no fruits. She was a "spreading vine" (10:1 NIV), but
now she is without fruit.[14] These agricultural images remind us that we
reap what we sow.

There's an interesting agricultural image in 10:4: "Therefore lawsuits
spring up like poisonous weeds in a plowed field" (NIV). People couldn't
trust one another, and few were keeping their promises; therefore, they had
to sue one another to get what they deserved. The multiplying of laws and
lawsuits is one evidence that integrity and credibility are vanishing from
society.

The final agricultural image is in verse 8: The idolatrous shrines will
become nothing but clumps and weeds, and the people will beg the Lord
to destroy them quickly (v. 8; see Luke 23:30; Rev. 6:16).

Twice in this passage, Hosea mentions "the days of Gibeah" (Hos.
9:9; 10:9). The reference is to the awful sins of the men of Gibeah and the

tragic civil war that followed (Judg. 19—21). The men of Gibeah practiced unnatural lust and killed an innocent woman in a gang rape episode. The city would not punish the offenders, so the whole nation attacked Benjamin and almost destroyed the tribe. In Hosea's day, all the ten tribes of Israel were practicing these abominable things, but God would judge them, and they would reap what they had sown.[15]

The chapter closes (Hos. 10:11–15) by comparing Israel to a young heifer that enjoys treading out the grain because she can eat and work at the same time. But then she is yoked to another beast and forced to do the hard work of plowing. Israel's "salad days" were over and she would feel the Assyrian yoke.

In verse 12, the prophet gives one more appeal to the nation to repent and seek the Lord. "Fallow ground" is land that has lain idle and become hard and full of weeds. This appeal sounds like the preaching of John the Baptist: "Repent! Bear fruits worthy of repentance!" (Matt. 3:1–12). The plow of conviction must first break up hard hearts before the seed of the Word can be planted and the gracious rain be sent from heaven.

The nation did not repent, and judgment fell. In 722 BC, the Assyrian army invaded the land, and the ten tribes as a nation vanished from the pages of history.[16]

"Righteousness exalts a nation, but sin is a reproach to any people" (Prov. 14:34 NKJV).

"Blessed is the nation whose God is the Lord" (Ps. 33:12 NKJV).

QUESTIONS FOR PERSONAL REFLECTION
OR GROUP DISCUSSION

1. Wiersbe says God wanted to forgive the Israelites and restore their fellowship with Him, but they weren't ready. What are some reasons why the Israelites wouldn't admit they had sinned? What makes a person or nation ready to return to the Lord?

2. How had the people of Israel reneged on their promises to God?

3. What was the result of their rejection of God's covenant?

4. What does it mean in 4:1 that there was no "knowledge of God in the land"? Why were the people responsible before God for this ignorance?

5. Why do you think the people of Israel turned to political maneuvering instead of repentance when they were in trouble? How do we do something similar today?

6. If, as Wiersbe states, the people "lacked the power to repent and turn back to God, for their sins had paralyzed them," how could they possibly avoid the coming judgment?

7. What are some experiences you have had in your walk with the Lord where you wanted to be rescued from suffering but not necessarily cleansed from your sin?

8. Hosea calls for a trumpet of alarm to be sounded so the Israelites could have one last chance to repent before the enemy came. What might sound the alarm for us personally? As a church? As a nation?

9. Hosea mentions the increase of lawsuits. Why would lawsuits be a sign of sin?

10. What are you reaping now from your sowing in younger years (good or bad)? What are you trying to sow now? What are you hoping to reap?

Chapter Three

LOVE SO AMAZING

(Hosea 11—14)

How could Hosea's unfaithful wife Gomer ever question her husband's love? Didn't he demonstrate it by seeking her out, pleading with her to come home, and paying the price to set her free?

How could Israel ever question God's love and refuse to respond to it? After all, the nation had not only broken the law of God; they had broken the heart of God. In the closing chapters of this book, Hosea reminded them of God's compassion for His people, and he did it by presenting three clear evidences of God's love.

1. GOD'S MERCIES IN THE PAST (11:1–12)

At least fourteen times in the book of Deuteronomy, Moses used the word *remember.* Deuteronomy is Moses' farewell address to the new generation of Israelites as they were preparing to enter the Promised Land. But why would Moses ask these young people to look back when they were getting ready to move forward? Because a correct understanding of God's dealings in the past is the best way to be certain of success in the future. Philosopher George Santayana expressed this truth succinctly: "Those who do not remember the past are condemned to relive it."[1]

God's love demonstrated at the exodus (vv. 1–2). God sent Joseph ahead into Egypt to prepare the way for Jacob and his sons. What Joseph's brothers did to their brother was meant for evil, but God used it for good (Gen. 50:20). Because of Joseph, the people of Israel were kept alive during the severe famine and were able to multiply in the ensuing years. From this humble beginning, God formed a nation; Moses led that nation out of Egypt in great power and triumph (Ex. 12—15).

Hosea pictures the God of the exodus as a tender Father who freed His son from bondage. The emphasis here is not on Israel the unfaithful wife, but on Israel the ungrateful son. (For God as "Father" and Israel as a "son," see Ex. 4:22–23; Isa. 1:2–4; Deut. 32:5). After all God did for His son, he will still refuse to return His love or obey His will.

God's love demonstrated in the wilderness (vv. 3–4). The loving Father not only carried His son out of bondage, but He also taught him to walk and tenderly cared for him during the wilderness journey. When a child stumbles and gets bruised, mother and father are there to give healing and encouragement, and that's what God did for His people. He taught them, healed them, and led them; He was careful to lead them as you would a child and not as you would an animal. He bound Himself to them with cords of love, not with bit and bridle (Ps. 32:8–9) or a galling yoke.

Read Hosea 11:1–4 again, but instead of noting what God did for Israel, notice how Israel treated God. Like spoiled children, they rebelled against their Father and turned to idols. God spoke to them through His prophets, but the more God called to Israel, the more they strayed from Him! They were happy to enjoy His gifts, but they didn't want to obey the Giver. He sought to lead them with ties of love, but they said, "Let us break their bands asunder, and cast away their cords from us" (Ps. 2:3).

Throughout history, whether Jewish or Gentile, human nature is pretty much the same, and all of us are prone to do what Israel did: enjoy God's blessings, but take God for granted. "My people are determined to turn from me" (Hos. 11:7 NIV). "Alas, sinful nation, a people laden with iniquity, a brood of evildoers, children who are corrupters!" (Isa. 1:4 NKJV). God set them free and guided them to their inheritance, but within one generation after the death of Joshua, the nation turned to idolatry and forsook the Lord (Judg. 2:7ff.).

God's love demonstrated by His long-suffering (vv. 5–7). On more than one occasion, God could have destroyed the nation and started over again (Ex. 32:10), but He chose to be long-suffering. When the journey became difficult, the Jews wanted to go back to Egypt; they complained when they should have been praying and giving thanks for God's mercies.

We have already seen that some of the references to Egypt in this book refer to the "new bondage" in Assyria (Hos. 11:5). Israel refused to repent, so the nation had to go into captivity. They made plans without consulting God, so their defenses would fall before the invaders. The only time they called on God was when they were in trouble, and God graciously helped them; but now the end had come.

God's love demonstrated by His faithfulness to His promises (vv. 8–9). What a revelation we have in 11:8 of the compassionate heart of God! According to Jewish law, a rebellious son was supposed to be turned over to the elders of the city and stoned to death (Deut. 21:18–21), but how could God do this to His beloved son, Israel? (Centuries later, His innocent, only begotten Son would suffer for the sins of the whole world.) God destroyed the cities of the plain because of their sins (Gen. 18:16—19:29), and those people didn't have the same privileges of learning about God that Israel had. What right did Israel have to expect God to spare them, especially since they were sinning against a flood of light?

What motivated God to spare Israel from total destruction? Not only His deep compassion, but also His faithfulness to His covenant. "For I am God, and not man" (Hos. 11:9). "God is not a man, that He should lie, nor a son of man, that He should repent. Has He said, and will He not do? Or has He spoken, and will He not make it good?" (Num. 23:19 NKJV).

God's covenant with Abraham (Gen. 12:1–3) is unconditional and will not change; therefore, the nation of Israel is preserved. But His covenant with Israel at Sinai had conditions attached, and if the people failed to meet those conditions, God was obligated to withdraw His blessings. Israel's possession of the land and its blessings is based on the Abrahamic covenant, but their enjoyment of the land and its blessings is based on the Mosaic covenant. God was faithful to both covenants: He preserved the nation, but He disciplined them for their sins.

God's love demonstrated by the hope of future restoration (vv. 10–12). Often in Scripture you will find a declaration of judgment immediately followed by a promise of hope, and that's the case here. Hosea looks ahead to the end times when Israel will be gathered together from all the nations, brought to their own land, cleansed of their sins, and established in their kingdom. In the past, God roared like a lion when He judged the nation (5:14; 13:7), but in the future, His "roar" will call His people to come back to their land. Like birds turned loose from their cages, the people of Israel will swiftly fly to their own land, and God will "settle them in their homes" (11:11 NIV).

Meanwhile, God is long-suffering with His people, as He is with all sinners (2 Peter 3:9), even though they lie to Him and rebel against Him (Hos. 11:12). What Jesus said to Jerusalem in His day, God was saying through Hosea to the people of that day: "How often I wanted to gather your children together, as a hen gathers her chicks under her wings, but you were not willing!" (Matt. 23:37 NKJV).

God's mercies in the past certainly proved His love, but Hosea offered a second evidence that God loved His people.

2. GOD'S DISCIPLINES IN THE PRESENT (12:1—13:16)

"For whom the Lord loves He chastens, and scourges every son whom He receives" (Heb. 12:6 NKJV; Prov. 3:11–12). Chastening isn't a judge inflicting punishment on a criminal in order to uphold the law. Rather, chastening is a loving parent disciplining his or her child in order to perfect his character and build his endurance.[2] Punishment has to do with law, which is important, but chastening has to do with love, which is also important.

The need for discipline (12:1). The Jewish people were living for vanity—"the wind"—and receiving no nourishment. The word translated "feed" means "to graze"; but whoever saw hungry sheep ignoring the green grass and chewing on the wind? The very idea is ridiculous, but that's the way God's people were living.

Israel was committing two sins: First, they were worshipping idols, which are nothing, even less than nothing, and turning from the true God to live on empty substitutes. They were feeding on the wind. Second, they were depending for protection on treaties with Egypt and Assyria instead of trusting their great God. This too was emptiness and chasing after the wind, and God had to discipline Israel to bring them back to Himself and His Word.

The example of discipline (12:2–6, 12). Abraham is the father of the Jewish nation (Matt. 3:9), but it was Jacob who built the twelve tribes of Israel (Gen. 46:8–27).[3] Hosea used the name "Jacob" for the nation because Jacob is an illustration of God's loving discipline. Hosea cited several key events in Jacob's life.

Jacob struggled with his brother even before he and Esau were born (25:20–23), and at birth, Jacob tried to trip up his brother Esau even as they were coming from the womb (vv. 24–26). The name "Jacob" means "he grasps the heel," which is another way of saying, "He's a deceiver, a trickster."[4] During most of his life, Jacob struggled with himself, with others, and with the Lord, and until he surrendered to God at Jabbok, he never really walked by faith. God had to discipline him to bring him to that place of surrender.

In obedience to God's command, Jacob left Shechem and went to Bethel (Gen. 35), for it was at Bethel that he had first met the Lord years before (28:10–22). There God had revealed Himself and given Jacob promises for himself and his descendants, and there Jacob had made solemn vows to the Lord. Actually, the return to Bethel was a new spiritual beginning for his whole family; for Jacob commanded them to abandon their foreign gods and worship Jehovah alone. It does a family good to experience this kind of dedication. Alexander Whyte said that the victorious Christian life is a series of new beginnings, and he was right.

But the Bethel experience also included some pain, for it was on that journey that Jacob's beloved wife Rachel died in giving birth to Benjamin (35:16–22). She called the boy Ben-Oni, which means "son of my sorrow"; but by faith, Jacob renamed him Benjamin, "son of my right hand."[5]

The divine title "Lord God of hosts [armies]" (Hos. 12:5) reminds us of Jacob's experience at Mahanaim when he was about to meet his brother Esau (Gen. 32). Mahanaim means "the two camps," for Jacob saw an army of angels watching over his camp. He was afraid of Esau and tried to appease him with gifts instead of trusting the Lord to deliver him. After all, didn't God promise to care for Jacob and bring him safely back to Bethel? It was there that the angel of God wrestled with Jacob and "broke" him.

Jacob's experiences getting a wife and raising a family are examples of God's loving discipline (Gen. 29—30). In order to get the family blessing, Jacob had schemed and lied to his father Isaac, but now Laban would scheme and lie to Jacob in order to marry off two daughters in one week! Trying to please two wives, only one of whom he really loved, and trying to raise a large family brought many burdens to Jacob, but he persisted, and God blessed him and made him a wealthy man. However, during those difficult years, Jacob suffered much (31:36–42), yet the Lord was working out His purposes.

The reasons for discipline (12:7—13:6). Now Hosea names some of the sins that his people had committed. Some of these he has dealt with before, so there's no need to discuss them in detail.

He begins with dishonesty in business (12:7), defrauding people so as to make more money. Their prosperity led to pride (v. 8), the kind of self-sufficiency that says, "We don't need God" (see Rev. 3:17). But the Lord warned that He would humble them. Instead of enjoying their houses, they would live in tents as they did during their wilderness journey. When the Assyrians were through with Israel, the Jews would be grateful even for the booths they lived in for a week during the Feast of Tabernacles.

The prophets God sent had warned the people, but the people wouldn't listen (Hos. 12:10). They turned from the Word of the living God and practiced idolatry (vv. 11–14). This provoked God to anger, and the way they shed innocent blood provoked Him even more. (On Gilead's wickedness, see 6:8–9.)

Hosea singled out the arrogant attitude of the tribe of Ephraim (13:1–3). The name "Ephraim" is found thirty-seven times in Hosea's prophecy. Sometimes "Ephraim" is a synonym for the whole northern kingdom, but here the prophet was addressing the tribe of Ephraim in particular. Ephraim and Manasseh were the sons of Joseph whom Jacob "adopted" and whose birth order he reversed (Gen. 48). Manasseh was the firstborn, but Jacob gave that honor to Ephraim.

The people of Ephraim felt they were an important tribe that deserved to be listened to and obeyed. After all, Joshua came from Ephraim (Num. 13:8) and so did the first king of the northern kingdom, Jeroboam I (1 Kings 11:26). The tabernacle of testimony was pitched in Shiloh, which was in Ephraim (Josh. 18:1). In their arrogance, the tribe of Ephraim created problems for both Gideon (Judg. 7:24–25; 8:1–3) and Jephthah (12:1–6). After the death of King Saul, the Ephraimites refused to submit to David's rule (2 Sam. 2:8–11); in fact, they had a strong prejudice against the tribe of Judah, the ruling tribe (2 Sam. 19:40–43). When the northern kingdom was established, so powerful were the Ephraimites that the kingdom was even called by their name.

But Ephraim abandoned Jehovah for Baal, and that brought spiritual death. They gladly participated in Jeroboam's man-made religion by sacrificing to the golden calves—even offering human sacrifices—and kissing the calves in worship. But idols are nothing, and those who worship them become like them—nothing (Ps. 115:8). Hosea compared the people to the "nothings" with which they were familiar: morning dew that the sun burns away; chaff that the wind blows away; and smoke that disappears out the window and is seen no more.

One more sin that Hosea condemned was the nation's ingratitude (Hos. 13:4–6). It was the same old story: The Jews were glad for what God had done for their forefathers—the exodus, God's provision and guidance in the wilderness, the abundant wealth in the Promised Land—but they didn't really show Him sincere appreciation. In their trials, they turned to God for help, but in their prosperity, they became proud and turned away from God to idols. Moses had warned them about this sin, but they committed it just the same (Deut. 8:10–20).

The name "Ephraim" means "fruitful," and this was a very fruitful tribe. Through Jacob, God had promised abundant blessings to Joseph and his sons (Gen. 48; 49:22–26), and that promise was fulfilled. It's too bad the people didn't use what God gave them for God's glory.

The kinds of discipline (13:7–16). Once again, Hosea uses a number of similes and metaphors to describe the trials that God was sending on His disobedient people. Like a ferocious beast, He would suddenly attack them (vv. 7–8; see 5:14), a reference to the invasion of the Assyrian army. The rulers of Israel would be weak, temporary, and ineffective (13:9–11; see 8:4). Now the time had come for the nation to have no king (3:4), a situation that would last for centuries.

The woman in travail is used often in Scripture to picture extreme pain and sorrow (13:13; Isa. 13:8; Jer. 4:31; Matt. 24:8), but Hosea adds a new twist. He sees the woman too weak to deliver the child, and the baby too stupid to come out of the womb! All the travail was wasted.

The invasion of the Assyrians will be like a hot, dry wind from the desert that will smother the people and dry up the watercourses. All the nation's treasures will be plundered, and their greatest treasure, their children, will be slain mercilessly. Why? Because the nation would not return to God.

Paul quoted Hosea 13:14 in 1 Corinthians 15:55 to emphasize the victory of Jesus Christ over death and the grave because of His resurrection, but Hosea's words in this context may have a different meaning.[6]

The next statement ("I will have no compassion" NIV) supports our interpretation that Hosea 13:14 refers to judgment and not victory over the enemy. This doesn't suggest that God no longer loved His people, because God's love for His people is the major theme of this book. But the time had come for God to discipline the nation, for they had rejected every other manifestation of His love. "For I will not relent!" is the way *The Living Bible* states it.

God revealed His love to Israel in His past mercies and now in His present disciplines. Hosea closes his book with a third evidence of God's love.

3. GOD'S PROMISES FOR THE FUTURE (14:1–9)

Though His people may turn away from Him, God will not abandon them, even though He disciplines them, for He is true to His covenant and His promises. "If we are faithless, He remains faithful; He cannot deny Himself" (2 Tim. 2:13 NKJV).

God pleads with His people to return to Him and forsake the sins that were causing their downfall (Hos. 14:1). He had already told them to plow up their hard hearts and seek the Lord (Hos. 10:12) and to turn to God for mercy (12:6), but now He talks to them like little children and tells them just what to do. The Lord gives them promises to encourage them to repent.

He will receive us (vv. 2–3). God had every reason to reject His sinful people, but He chose to offer them forgiveness. Instead of bringing sacrifices, they needed to bring sincere words of repentance and ask God for His gracious forgiveness. "For You do not desire sacrifice, or else I would give it; You do not delight in burnt offering. The sacrifices of God are a broken spirit, a broken and a contrite heart—these, O God, You will not despise" (Ps. 51:16–17 NKJV).

He will restore us (v. 4). God restores the penitent to spiritual health and heals their backsliding (Jer. 14:7). When a person collapses with sickness, it's usually the result of a process that's been working in the body for weeks or months. First an infection gets into the system and begins to grow. The person experiences weariness and loss of appetite, then weakness, and then the collapse occurs. When sin gets into the inner person and isn't dealt with, it acts like an insidious infection: It grows quietly; it brings loss of spiritual appetite; it creates weariness and weakness; and then comes the collapse.

For example, when Peter denied his Lord three times, that sin didn't suddenly appear; it was the result of gradual spiritual deterioration. The denial began with Peter's pride, when he told the Lord he would never forsake Him and would even die for Him. The next stage was sleeping when he should have been praying, and then fighting when he should have put away his sword. Peter should have left the scene ("I will smite the shepherd, and the sheep of the flock shall be scattered abroad" [Matt. 26:31; Zech. 13:7]); but instead, he followed to see what would happen and walked right into temptation.

When we confess our sins to the Lord, He forgives us and the "germs of sin" are cleansed away (1 John 1:9), but, as with physical sickness, often there's a period of recuperation when we get back our strength and our appetite for spiritual food. "I will love them freely" describes that period, when we're back in fellowship with the Lord and enjoying His presence. We see the smile of His face, for His anger is turned away.

He will revive us (vv. 5–8). Hosea pictures the restoration of the penitent as the emergence of new life in a dry field on which the refreshing dew has fallen.[7] In the summer and early autumn in the Holy Land, the dew is very heavy and greatly appreciated (Ps. 133:3; Isa. 18:4). That's what the word *revive* means: to bring new life. The rich vegetation appears, producing beauty and fragrance where once the farmer saw only ugliness and emptiness. The fallow ground becomes a fruitful garden!

The closing verse presents us with only two alternatives: rebel against the Lord and continue to stumble, or return to the Lord and walk securely in His ways. The first choice is foolish; the second choice is wise.

"I have set before you life and death, blessing and cursing: therefore choose life" (Deut. 30:19).

QUESTIONS FOR PERSONAL REFLECTION
OR GROUP DISCUSSION

1. What makes confession of sin (to God or other people) so difficult? What makes it easier?

2. Of the descriptions of God's actions in 11:3–4, which is most touching to you? How does this picture fit with the terrible judgment from God that the Israelites suffered at the hands of the Assyrians?

3. In what ways have you enjoyed the blessings of God but have then taken the Giver for granted? What reminds you to give thanks?

4. How is it possible for us to stay away from the horrendous sin and apathy that brought the Israelites down? What do we have that they did not?

5. One reason for judgment that the prophets speak of again and again is dishonesty in business (12:7). Why is that as serious a sin as idolatry?

6. God wanted to gather His people to Himself, but they maintained their distance. Why are we today also often not willing to be drawn close to the Lord?

7. How do people in our society "feed on wind"? What ideas do you have to help them see the futility of their "feeding"? What are they actually hungry for?

8. Why are words so important in genuine repentance (14:2)? What else is important, and why?

9. Israel had to admit, "Assyria cannot save us" (14:3 NIV). When have you had to admit, "_____ cannot save me"?

10. What sentence in Hosea 14 is most encouraging to you, and why?

JOEL IN HIS TIME

Each prophet had his own unique approach to his own special message. Hosea's message was an application of his sad domestic trials, emphasizing God's jealous love, but Joel's message was an interpretation of a national calamity—a plague of locusts and a drought—and emphasized God's glorious kingdom.

Joel may well have been the first of the writing prophets; he probably ministered in Judah during the reign of King Joash (835–796 BC). You find the record in 2 Kings 11—12 and 2 Chronicles 22—24. Joash came to the throne at the age of seven, and Jehoiada the priest was his mentor. This may explain why Joel says nothing about the king, since Joash was learning the job.

Joel's major theme is the "day of the Lord" and the need for God's people to be prepared. "Day of the Lord" is used in Scripture to refer to different periods when God sent judgment to His people,[1] but the main emphasis is on the *future* "day of the Lord" when the nations will be judged and Christ shall return to set up His glorious kingdom.

Joel refers to three important events, each of which he calls a "day of the Lord." He sees the plague of locusts as an *immediate* day of the Lord (Joel 1:1–20), the invasion of Judah by Assyria as an *imminent* day of the

Lord (2:1–27), and the final judgment of the world as the *ultimate* day of the Lord (2:28—3:21). In the first, the locusts are a metaphorical army; in the second, the locusts symbolize a real army; in the third, the locusts aren't seen at all, and the armies are very real and very dangerous.

A SUGGESTED OUTLINE OF THE BOOK OF JOEL

Theme: "The Day of the Lord" (1:15; 2:1, 11, 31; 3:14)

Key verses: Joel 2:12–13

I. The Immediate Day of the Lord (Joel 1:1–20)

    1. Hear! (elders, citizens) (Joel 1:2–4)

    2. Wake up! (drunkards) (Joel 1:5–7)

    3. Mourn! (farmers) (Joel 1:8–12)

    4. Call a fast! (priests) (Joel 1:13–20)

II. The Imminent Day of the Lord (Joel 2:1–27)[1]

    1. The invading army, like locusts (Joel 2:1–11)

    2. The call to repent (Joel 2:12–17)

    3. The promise of restoration (Joel 2:18–27)

III. The Ultimate Day of the Lord (Joel 2:28—3:21)

    1. *Before* that day—Spirit poured out (Joel 2:28–32)

    2. *During* that day—judgment poured out (Joel 3:1–16)

    3. *After* that day—blessing poured out (Joel 3:17–21)

Chapter Four

WATCHING THE DAY OF THE LORD

(Joel 1—2:27)

If there had been newspapers in Joel's day, the headlines might have read

LOCUSTS INVADE THE LAND!
NATION FACES SEVERE ECONOMIC CRISIS
No End to Drought in Sight

A wise preacher or teacher will get the people's attention by referring to something they're all concerned about. In this case, the people of Judah were talking about the economic crisis, so the Lord led Joel to use that event as the background for his messages. The people didn't realize it, but they were watching the day of the Lord unfold before their very eyes, and the prophet Joel explained it to them.

The name "Joel" means "the Lord is God." Like all true prophets, Joel was commissioned to call the people back to the worship of the true God; and he did this by declaring "the word of the Lord" (1:1; see Jer. 1:2; Ezek. 1:3; and the first verses of Hosea, Micah, Zephaniah, Haggai, Zechariah, and Malachi). It was the task of the priests to teach the people the law, and it was the responsibility of the prophets to call the people back to the Lord whenever they strayed from His law. The prophets also interpreted historical events in the light of the Word of God to help the people understand God's will for their lives. They were "forth-tellers" as well as "foretellers."

Joel wanted the people of Judah to understand what God was saying to them through the plague and the drought. In our own times, the nations of the world are experiencing severe droughts and famines, frightening epidemics, unexpected earthquakes, devastating floods, and other "natural disasters," all of which have greatly affected national and global economies; yet very few people have asked, "What is God saying to us?" Joel wrote his book so the people would know what God was saying through these critical events.

As you can see from the suggested outline of Joel's book, the prophet announced "the day of the Lord" and applied it to three events: the plague of locusts, the future invasion of the Assyrians, and the distant judgment that the Lord would send on the whole world. In this chapter, we want to focus on the first two applications of "the day of the Lord."

The Immediate Day of the Lord (1:1–20)

When you're in a crisis, you'll hear all kinds of voices interpreting what's going on and telling you what to do. The optimists will say, "This crisis isn't going to last. Be brave!" The pessimists will sob, "It's going to get worse and there's no escape! We're done for!" The alarmists will see the enemy behind every tree, and the scoffers will question the news reports and shrug their shoulders, saying, "What difference does it make anyway?"

But Joel was a realist who looked at life from the standpoint of the Word of the Lord. He addressed himself to five groups of citizens and gave them four admonitions from the Lord.

(1) The elders and citizens in general: "Hear this!" (vv. 2–4). He addressed the old men[1] first for probably two reasons: they had long experience and could authenticate what he was saying, and they were respected citizens in the land. With their support, Joel wasn't just a voice crying in the wilderness. They agreed with the prophet that the nation faced a catastrophe of monumental proportion such as they had never seen before. It was something people would tell to their children and grandchildren for years to come.

Joel used four different words to describe the plague (Joel 1:4; see 2:25), and it's been suggested that they represent four stages in the life cycle of the locusts. However, the words probably convey the idea of successive swarms of locusts invading the land, each swarm destroying what the others had left behind. A swarm of locusts can devastate the vegetation of a countryside with amazing rapidity and thoroughness, and nothing can stop them (Ex. 10:1–20).

(2) To the drunkards: "Wake up and weep!" (vv. 5–7). Except for pointing out the insincerity of some of the worshippers (2:12–13), drunkenness is the only sin that Joel actually names in his book. However, this was a serious sin that the prophets often condemned (Hos. 7:5; Amos 4:1). Perhaps the drunkards represented all the careless people in the land whose only interest was sinful pleasure.

These people had good reason to weep because there was no wine and wouldn't be any more until the next season, if there was a next season. Because of the locusts and the drought, "the new wine is dried up … the vine is dried up" (Joel 1:10, 12). Keep in mind that bread and wine were staples in the Jewish diet, so that even the people who didn't get drunk were affected by the loss.

Joel compared the locusts to an invading nation and to hungry lions with sharp teeth (v. 6; see 2:2, 11). They attacked the vines and the fig trees, two things essential to Jewish life. Having one's own vineyard and fig trees was a symbol of success and contentment in the East (2:22; Isa. 36:16; Amos 4:9; Ps. 105:33). Note how Joel uses the personal pronoun "my" as he speaks of the land and its vegetation, for all of it belonged to the Lord, and He had a right to do with it whatever He pleased.

(3) To the farmers: "Despair and wail!" (vv. 8–12). Joel named some of the crops that had been ruined: the grain (wheat and barley), the new wine, the oil, and the fruit from the pomegranate, palm, and apple trees. From season to season, the locusts ate whatever was produced, and the drought kept the soil from producing anything more. In verses 18–20, Joel includes the flocks and herds and their pastures. All that the farmers could do was express their grief and lament like an engaged girl whose fiancé had died. It seemed a hopeless situation.

(4) To the priests: "Call a fast!" (vv. 13–20). Not only were the people in need, but so was the temple. Nobody could bring the proper sacrifices because no meal, wine, or animals were available. Joel called the priests to lament and pray, including those who worked "the night shift" (Ps. 134:1).[2]

The Jews were required to observe only one fast, and that was on the annual Day of Atonement (Lev. 16:29, 31). But the religious leaders could call a fast whenever the people faced an emergency and needed to humble themselves and seek God's face (Judg. 20:26; 2 Chron. 20:3; Ezra 8:21; Neh. 9:1–3; Jer. 36:9). This was such an emergency. "Gird yourself" (Joel 1:13) means "Put on sackcloth!" (See Jer. 4:8; 6:26.) It was time for the people to humble themselves and pray (2 Chron. 7:14).

In Joel 1:15–18, we have the lament of the nation, and in verses 19–20, the prayer of the prophet as he interceded for the nation. The lament is a vivid description of the sad condition of the land, the crops, the flocks, and the herds; for "the day of the Lord" had come to the nation. The immediate reference is to the assault of the locusts and the devastating effects of the drought, but later, Joel uses the phrase to describe the terrible "day of the Lord" when the nations will be judged. God is the Lord of creation, and without His blessing, nature cannot produce what we need for sustaining life (Ps. 65; 104:10–18, 21; 145:15). We should never pray lightly, "Give us this day our daily bread," for only God can sustain life (Acts 17:25, 28).

"How the cattle moan!" (Joel 1:18 NIV). This reminds us that all creation "groans and labors" because of the bondage of sin in the world (Rom. 8:18–22; Gen. 3:17–19). Creation longs for that day when the Creator will return to earth and set it free from sin's shackles, and then "the wilderness and the solitary place shall be glad … and the desert shall rejoice, and blossom as the rose" (Isa. 35:1).

It wasn't enough for the people to humble themselves and lament; they also had to pray. This is what God required in His covenant with His people (2 Chron. 6:26–27; 7:12–15; see Deut. 28:23–24). Joel didn't ask God for anything; he simply told the Lord of the suffering of the land, the beasts, and the people, knowing that God would do what was right. "The fire" (Joel 1:20) refers to the drought, which left the land looking like it had been burned.

Too often we drift along from day to day, taking our blessings for granted, until God permits a natural calamity to occur and remind us of our total dependence on Him. When water is rationed and food is scarce, and when prices for necessities escalate, then we discover the poverty of our artificial civilization and our throwaway society. Suddenly, necessities become luxuries, and luxuries become burdens.

God didn't have to send great battalions to Judah to bring the people to their knees. All He needed was a swarm of little insects, and they did the job. Sometimes He uses bacteria or viruses so tiny that you need a special microscope to see them. He is the "Lord of hosts," the Lord of the armies of heaven and earth. He is "the Almighty" (v. 15) and none can stay His powerful hand.[3]

THE IMMINENT DAY OF THE LORD (2:1–27)

Now that he had their attention, Joel told the people to stop looking around at the locusts and to start looking ahead to the fulfillment of what the locust plague symbolized: the invasion of a fierce army from the north (v. 20). Unless Joel had some other attack in mind, about which we know nothing, he was probably referring to the Assyrian invasion, during the reign of King Hezekiah, which took place in 701 BC (Isa. 36—37). God allowed the Assyrians to ravage the land, but He miraculously delivered Jerusalem from being taken captive.[4] The prophet gave the people three timely instructions.

(1) "Blow the trumpet!" (vv. 1–11). This was real war, so Joel commanded the watchmen to blow their trumpets and warn the people. The Jews used trumpets to call assemblies, announce special events, mark religious festivals, and warn the people that war had been declared (Num. 10; Jer. 4:5; 6:1; Hos. 5:8). In this case, they blew the trumpet to announce war and to call a fast (Joel 2:15). Their weapons against the invading enemy would be repentance and prayer; the Lord would fight for them.

Twice in this passage, Joel tells us that invasion is "the day of the Lord" (vv. 1, 11), meaning a very special period that God had planned and would direct. "The Lord thunders at the head of his army" (v. 11 NIV). It was God who brought the locusts of the land and God would allow the Assyrians to invade the land (Isa. 7:17–25; 8:7). He would permit them to ravage Judah just as the locusts had done, only the Assyrians would also abuse and kill people. "Woe to Assyria, the rod of My anger and the staff in whose hand is My indignation. I will send him against an ungodly nation ... to seize the spoil, to take the prey, and to tread them down like the mire of the streets" (Isa. 10:5–6 NKJV).

In his vivid account of the invading army, Joel sees them coming in great hordes, "like dawn spreading across the mountains" (Joel 2:2 NIV). Once again, he uses the locusts to describe the soldiers. Just as the locusts had destroyed everything edible before them, so the army would use a "scorched earth policy" and devastate the towns and the land (Isa. 36:10; 37:11–13, 18). The locusts looked like miniature horses, but the Assyrians would ride real horses and conquer the land.[5]

The prophet makes it clear that the Lord will be in charge of this invasion; this is His army fulfilling His Word (Joel 2:11). God can use even heathen nations to accomplish His purposes on this earth (Isa. 10:5–7; Jer. 25:9). The awesome cosmic disturbances described in Joel 2:10 are Joel's way of announcing that the Lord is in charge, for these signs accompany "the day of the Lord" (3:15; see Zeph. 1:14).

(2) "Rend your hearts!" (vv. 12–17). Once again, Joel called for a solemn assembly where God's people would repent of their sins and seek the Lord's help. The nation didn't know when this invasion would occur, so the important thing was for them to turn to the Lord now. But they must be sincere. It's easy to participate in a religious ceremony, tear your garments, and lament, but quite something else to humbly confess your sins and bring to God a repentant heart (Matt. 15:8–9). "The sacrifices of God are a broken spirit, a broken and a contrite heart—these, O God, You will not despise" (Ps. 51:17 NKJV).

The one thing that encourages us to repent and return to the Lord is the character of God. Knowing that He is indeed "gracious and compassionate, slow to anger and abounding in love" (Joel 2:13 NIV) ought to motivate us to seek His face. This description of the attributes of God goes back to Moses' meeting with the Lord on Mount Sinai, when he interceded for the sinful nation of Israel (Ex. 34:6–7). You find echoes of it in Numbers 14:18 (another scene of Moses' intercession); Nehemiah 9:17; Psalms 86:15, 103:8, and 145:8; and Jonah 4:2. Such a gracious God would "turn and have pity" (Joel 2:14 NIV).[6] Note that Joel's concern was that the people would once again have offerings to bring to the Lord, not just food on their tables.

But all the people must assemble and then turn to the Lord (vv. 15–17). This includes elders and children, nursing babies and priests, and even the newlyweds who were not supposed to be disturbed during their first year of marriage, not even because of war (Deut. 24:5). The prophet even gave them a prayer to use (Joel 2:17) that presents two reasons why God should deliver them: (1) Israel's covenant privileges as God's heritage and (2) the glory of God's name before the other nations. Moses used these same arguments when he pled for the people (Ex. 32:11–13; 33:12–23).

The Jews are indeed God's special treasure and heritage (Ex. 15:17; 19:5–6; Ps. 94:5; Jer. 2:7; 12:7–9). To Israel, He gave His laws, His covenants, the temple and priesthood, a special land, and the promise that they would bless the whole world (Gen. 12:1–3; Rom. 9:1–5). From Israel came the written Word of God and the gift of the Savior (John 4:22).

Israel was called to bear witness to the other nations that their God was the only true God. How could God be glorified if His people were destroyed and the pagans could gleefully ask, "Where is their God?" (See Ps. 79:10; 115:2; also Mic. 7:10.) The nation had to choose between revival (getting right with God) or reproach (robbing God of glory).

(3) "Believe His promises!" (vv. 18–27). Joel now looks beyond the invasion to the time when God would heal His land and restore His blessings to His people. Just as He blew the locusts into the depths of the Dead Sea and the Mediterranean Sea (eastern and western seas), so He could drive the invading army out of the land. In one night, God killed 185,000 Assyrian soldiers, and Sennacherib went home a defeated king (Isa. 37:36–38). The corpses must have created quite a stench before they were buried.

Some Bible scholars believe that Psalm 126 grew out of this event, for it describes a sudden and surprising deliverance that startled the nation. (Judah's return from Babylonian captivity was neither sudden or surprising.) "The Lord hath done great things for us; whereof we are glad" (v. 3) is echoed in Joel 2:21: "Be glad and rejoice; for the Lord will do great things." Both Joel 2:23–27 and Psalm 126:5–6 describe the restoration of the ravaged earth and the return of the harvests. This fulfilled what Isaiah promised to King Hezekiah (Isa. 37:30).

Without the former rain (March–April) and the latter rain (October–November), the land could not bear its crops; and one way God disciplined

His people was to shut off the rain (Deut. 11:13–17). But the Lord promised to give such bumper crops that the harvest would more than compensate for all the people lost during the locust plague and the drought. "I will repay you for the years the locusts have eaten" (Joel 2:25 NIV) is a word of promise to all who return to the Lord with sincere and broken hearts.

"You cannot have back your time," said Charles Spurgeon, "but there is a strange and wonderful way in which God can give back to you the wasted blessings, the unripened fruits of years over which you mourned. … It is a pity that they should have been locust-eaten by your folly and negligence; but if they have been so, be not hopeless concerning them."[7]

And why will God do this for His deserving people? So that they will praise His name and never again be shamed before the heathen. "Then you will know that I am in Israel, that I am the Lord your God, and that there is no other; never again will my people be shamed" (v. 27 NIV).[8]

As never before, our lands today need healing. They are polluted by the shedding of innocent blood and the exploiting of both resources and people. We can claim God's promise in 2 Chronicles 7:14 because we are "His people."

QUESTIONS FOR PERSONAL REFLECTION
OR GROUP DISCUSSION

1. What are the three important events that for Joel were all "the day of the Lord"?

2. Until Joel interpreted it, God's people did not realize that they were witnessing the day of the Lord during the locust invasion. How did Joel know how to interpret this event of nature as a day when God was acting?

3. What interpretations have you heard from Christians today concerning the condition of our nation or world and what God is doing or is planning to do about it? Try to include interpretations from optimists and pessimists and the Scripture used to support the interpretations.

4. Who are the people today most likely to accept someone issuing an urgent warning of impending calamity? Who are the most reluctant to believe? Which are you?

5. Wiersbe suggests, "Perhaps the drunkards [in 1:5] represented all the careless people in the land whose only interest was sinful pleasure." Should such careless people weep today? Explain.

6. What was the purpose of the fast? If you have ever fasted, why did you do it and what was the outcome? What would be a substitute for sackcloth and ashes today?

7. What natural calamities or troubles have reminded you of your total dependence on God?

8. If God plans and directs each "day of the Lord," such as the Assyrians' attack, do you think God makes militaries attack? Or does He just permit them to go ahead? How can attackers like the Assyrians be held responsible even when they are used to accomplish God's purposes (see Isa. 10:5–9)?

9. How does knowing the character of God (Joel 2:13) affect your repentance (see also 1 John 1:9)?

10. Referring to the quote by Spurgeon near the end of the chapter, what are some personal or secondhand examples of mercifully getting repaid "for the years the locusts have eaten" (Joel 2:25 NIV)? To whom would this message bring hope and comfort?

11. If 2 Chronicles 7:14 applies the country you live in, what would that nation look like if it were "healed"?

Chapter Five

EXPECTING THE DAY OF THE LORD

(Joel 2:28—3:21)

J oel's message to Judah (and to us) is reaching its conclusion. He has described the immediate "day of the Lord," the terrible plague of the locusts. This led to a description of the imminent "day of the Lord," the impending invasion of the northern army. All that remains is for him to describe the ultimate "day of the Lord" when God will judge all the nations of the earth. "For the day of the Lord is near upon all the heathen" (Obad. 15).

Joel describes a sequence of events relating to this "great and terrible day of the Lord" (Joel 2:31), what will happen before that day, during that day, and after that day.

BEFORE THAT DAY: THE SPIRIT POURED OUT (2:28–32)

In the Hebrew Scriptures, these five verses form chapter 3 of Joel's prophecy; and chapter 4 in the Hebrew Scriptures is chapter 3 in the English Bible. The Jewish scholars who arranged the Old Testament Scriptures evidently thought that this paragraph was important enough to warrant a chapter by itself. However, now that we have a completed Bible, this important passage must be studied both in its Jewish context and in the context of the New Testament church.

The Jewish context. The "afterward" in 2:28 refers to the events described in 2:18–27 when the Lord heals the nation after the Assyrian invasion. However, it doesn't necessarily mean immediately afterward, for many centuries passed before the Spirit was poured out. When Peter quoted this verse in his sermon on the day of Pentecost, the Holy Spirit led him to interpret "afterward" to mean "in the last days" (Acts 2:17).

"The last days" began with the ministry of Christ on earth (Heb. 1:2) and will conclude with "the day of the Lord," that period of worldwide judgment that is also called "the tribulation" (Matt. 24:21, 29) and "the time of Jacob's trouble" (Jer. 30:7). Many students of prophecy think that this special time is detailed in Revelation 6—19, climaxing with the return of Christ to earth to deliver Israel and establish His kingdom (Isa. 2:2–5; Zech. 12—14; Rev. 19:11—20:6).[1]

Joel promised that before the "day of the Lord" begins, there will be a remarkable outpouring of the Holy Spirit accompanied by signs in the heavens and on the earth. During the Old Testament era, the Holy Spirit was given only to special people who had special jobs to do, like Moses and the prophets (Num. 11:17), the judges (Judg. 3:10; 6:34; 11:29), and great men like David (1 Sam. 16:13). But the promise God gave through Joel declared that the Spirit will come upon "all flesh," which includes men and women, young and old, Jew and Gentile. "And it shall come to pass that whoever calls on the name of the Lord shall be saved" (Joel 2:32 NKJV; see Acts 2:39).

The church context. In Acts 2, Peter did not say that Joel's prophecy was being fulfilled. He said that the same Holy Spirit Joel wrote about ("this is that") had now come and was empowering the believers to praise God in various languages understood by the Jews who were assembled in Jerusalem from many parts of the Roman Empire (Acts 2:5–12). In his prophecy, Joel promised "wonders in the heavens and in the earth, blood, and fire, and pillars of smoke. The sun … turned into darkness, and the moon into blood"

(Joel 2:30–31), but there is no record that any of these things occurred at Pentecost. The miracle that fascinated the crowd was the miracle of the tongues, not remarkable signs of nature.[2]

Furthermore, Joel's promise included a much wider audience than the one Peter addressed at Pentecost. Peter's audience was made up of men (Acts 2:22, 29) who were either Jews or Gentile proselytes to Judaism (v. 11). The Gentiles didn't enter into the blessing of the Spirit until Cornelius and his family and friends were converted (Acts 10—11). Peter used Joel's prophecy to declare that the promised Spirit had come and this was why the believers, men and women (1:14), were praising God in such an ecstatic manner. Peter was answering the accusation that the believers were drunk (2:13–16) and backing up his defense from the Scriptures.[3]

When it comes to Israel, "the last days" (or "latter times") will involve both tribulation and exaltation (Isa. 2:1–5; Mic. 4:1–5), a time of trouble followed by a time of triumph and glory. As far as the church is concerned, "the last days" involve "perilous times" of satanic opposition in the world and apostasy in the church (1 Tim. 4:1–5; 2 Tim. 3:1–8; 2 Peter 3:1–9; 1 John 2:18–23; Jude 18–19). Many Christians believe that during those trying "last days," the Lord will send a great moving of His Spirit, and many sinners will turn to the Savior before the awful "day of the Lord" is ushered in.

Certainly the church today needs a new filling of the Spirit of God. Apart from the ministry of the Spirit, believers can't witness with power (Acts 1:8), understand the Scriptures (John 16:13), glorify Christ (v. 14), pray in the will of God (Rom. 8:26–27), or develop Christian character (Gal. 5:22–23). We need to be praying for revival, a deeper working of the Spirit in His people, leading to confession of sin, repentance, forgiveness, and unity.

DURING THE DAY: JUDGMENT POURED OUT (3:1–16)

The phrase "bring again the captivity" (3:1) means "reverse the fortunes" or "restore the fortunes" (NIV). Because of the judgments set during the "day of the Lord," Israel's situation in the world will be dramatically changed, and God will deal justly with the nations of the world for the way they have treated His people Israel. Joel gives three important announcements.

(1) **"Nations, prepare for judgment!" (vv. 1–8).** This great battle will take place in the Valley of Jehoshaphat (vv. 2, 12), a site mentioned nowhere else in Scripture. In verse 14, it's called "the valley of decision," referring to God's decision (decree) to punish the nations.[4] Since the name "Jehoshaphat" means "the Lord judges," the name "Valley of Jehoshaphat" might well be symbolic, but some students believe it refers to the Plain of Esdraelon where the "battle of Armageddon" will be fought (Rev. 16:16).

Joel lists some of the sins that the Gentiles have committed against the Jews: scattering them among the nations; selling them into slavery; treating them like cheap merchandise for which people cast lots; plundering the land of its wealth; and taking what belonged to the Lord and using it for their own gods. Of course, many of the tragic experiences that came to the Jewish people were disciplines from God because they had violated His covenant, but the Gentile nations went beyond discipline to exploitation. Jeremiah said to the Babylonians, "You rejoice and are glad, you who pillage my inheritance, because you frolic like a heifer threshing grain and neigh like stallions" (Jer. 50:11 NIV).

It's worth noting that God refers to the Jews as "my people" and to the land as "my land." The wealth is "my silver and my gold." Even though the Jews have not obeyed the covenant or sought to please the Lord, He has not abandoned them. Even when they rejected their Messiah, God was merciful to them. He has preserved them as a nation and will one day come to their aid and defeat their enemies.

(2) **"Nations, prepare for war!" (vv. 9–15).** This passage describes what is generally called "the battle of Armageddon," when the armies of the nations unite against the Lord and His Christ (Ps. 2:1–3) and gather to destroy Jerusalem (Joel 3:16; Zech. 12—14). Joel compares the battle to the

harvesting of grain and grapes, when God will defeat the enemy as easily as a farmer wields a sickle or plucks grapes and crushes them to make wine (Joel 3:13). You will find a similar image in Revelation 14:14–20, when God reaps "the harvest of the earth" and "the vine of the earth" and crushes armies like clusters of grapes.

Frightening signs from the Lord will accompany this battle (Joel 3:15; see 2:10, 30–31), signs that Jesus mentioned in His prophetic discourse on the Mount of Olives (Matt. 24:29–31; Mark 13:19–27; Luke 21:25–28). Jesus taught that these signs would prepare the way for His personal coming to earth when He will defeat Israel's enemies, cleanse His people, and establish His kingdom (Zech. 12—14; Rev. 19:11ff.).

Joel 3:10 commands the nations to arm for battle, even to the point of turning farm tools into weapons, but Isaiah 2:4 and Micah 4:3 describe a different scene: "They shall beat their swords into plowshares, and their spears into pruninghooks" (Isa. 2:4). But Isaiah and Micah are describing the future kingdom, when people will learn war no more and no longer need weapons; while Joel is describing the battle that ushers in that peaceful kingdom.

(3) "Nations, prepare for defeat!" (v. 16). The name "Armageddon" is found only in Revelation 16:16, referring to the Plain of Esdraelon, where many major battles were fought in Old Testament times. Revelation 16:13–16 informs us that Satan, through his demonic powers, gathers the armies of the nations to fight against God at Jerusalem. But the invasion will fail, because Jesus will return in power and slaughter the enemy, turning the whole "battle" into a supper of flesh for the scavengers of the earth (19:17–19).

Like a fierce lion, God will "roar out of Zion" and conquer the enemy (see Amos 1:2, Hos. 11:10–11). When the Lamb becomes a Lion, the nations had better tremble (Rev. 5:5). The lost nations of the earth will perish when He utters His voice in judgment, but to His own people the Lord will be a refuge and a stronghold. "Come, my people, enter your chambers, and shut your doors behind you; hide yourself, as it were, for a little moment, until the indignation is past. For behold, the Lord comes out of His place to punish the inhabitants of the earth for their iniquity" (Isa. 26:20–21 NKJV).[5]

A Jewish proverb says, "No misfortune avoids a Jew." No people have suffered more at the hands of their fellow men than have the Jews. Pharaoh tried to drown the Jews, but instead, his own army was drowned by God (Ex. 14—15). Balaam tried to curse the Jews, but God turned the curse into a blessing (Num. 22:25; Deut. 23:5; Neh. 13:2). The Assyrians and Babylonians captured the Jews and put them in exile, but both of those great kingdoms are no more, while the Jews are still with us. Haman tried to exterminate the Jews, but he and his sons ended up hanging on the gallows (the book of Esther). Nebuchadnezzar put three Jews into a fiery furnace, only to discover that their God was with them and was able to deliver them (Dan. 3).

My friend the late Dr. Jacob Gartenhaus, gifted missionary to his own people, used to say, "We Jews are waterproof and fireproof; God has blessed us so that nobody can successfully curse us, and we shall be here long after our enemies have perished." God knows what the nations have done to the Jews, and He will one day settle accounts. Meanwhile, believers must pray for the peace of Jerusalem (Ps. 122:6) and lovingly witness to them in word and deed that Jesus is indeed their Messiah and Lord.

AFTER THAT DAY: BLESSING POURED OUT (3:17–21)

Everything will change when the King comes back and begins His reign! Joel promises a Holy City, a restored land, a cleansed people, and a glorious King.

A Holy City (v. 17). When Solomon dedicated the temple, the glory of the Lord came down and filled the building (1 Kings 8:10–11; 2 Chron. 5:11–14). Mount Zion, on which Jerusalem was built and the temple stood, was a very special place to the Jews because it was the place God chose for His own dwelling (Ps. 48; 87; 132:13). When the Babylonians destroyed the temple, the Jews prayed for the time when their temple would be restored and God's glory would return. "For God will save Zion, and will build the cities of Judah: that they may dwell there, and have it in possession" (69:35).

Today, the Jewish people have no temple on Mount Zion; instead, a mosque stands there. But God promises that He will restore Zion and dwell there in all His glory. "For the Lord shall comfort Zion: he will comfort all her waste places; and he will make her wilderness like Eden, and her desert like the garden of the Lord; joy and gladness shall be found therein, thanksgiving, and the voice of melody" (Isa. 51:3). The prophets anticipate that great day when "sorrow and mourning shall flee away" (v. 11) and God will once again dwell with His people (see Isa. 12; 33:20–24; 35; 52; Jer. 31; Mic. 4; Zech. 1).

Jerusalem is called "the Holy City" at least eight times in Scripture (Neh. 11:1, 18; Isa. 48:2; 52:1; Dan. 9:24; Matt. 4:5; 27:53; Rev. 11:2), and we still call it "the Holy City" today. Like every other city in this world, Jerusalem is inhabited by sinners who do sinful things. But the day will come when Jerusalem shall be cleansed (Zech. 13:1) and truly become a Holy City dedicated to the Lord (Isa. 4:1–6).

A restored land (vv. 18–19). Over the centuries, the land of Israel has been ravaged by wars, famines, droughts, and the invasions of marauding insects such as Joel wrote about in the first chapter of his book, but there is coming a day when the land will be like the Garden of Eden for beauty and fruitfulness. "He will make her deserts like Eden, her wastelands like the garden of the Lord" (Isa. 51:3 NIV).

In the first chapter of Joel's prophecy, the people were wailing because they had no food, but that will not happen when God restores His people and their land. It will not only be a "land of milk and honey," but it will have plenty of wine and water as well. The land of Israel has always depended on the early and latter rains for water, but God will give them fountains and a river to water the land.

Jerusalem is the only city of antiquity that wasn't built near a great river. Rome had the Tiber; Nineveh was built near the Tigris and Babylon on the Euphrates; and the great Egyptian cities were built near the Nile. But in the kingdom, Jerusalem will have a river that proceeds from the temple of God. "On that day living water will flow out from Jerusalem, half to the eastern sea [the Dead Sea] and half to the western sea [the Mediterranean], in summer and in winter" (Zech. 14:8 NIV). You find this river and its special blessings described in Ezekiel 47.

In contrast to the land of Israel, the lands of their enemies, Egypt and Edom, will be desolate as a punishment for the way they treated the Jewish people. This means that Egypt and Edom will have to depend on Israel for the basic things of life, such as food and water.

A cleansed people (vv. 20–21a). What good would it be to have a restored land if it were populated with a sinful people? God's people must be cleansed before they can enter into the promised kingdom. God promises to cleanse His people of their sins, forgive them, and restore them to Himself. "In that day there shall be a fountain opened to the house of David and to the inhabitants of Jerusalem for sin and for uncleanness" (Zech. 13:1).

The prophet Ezekiel describes this cleansing: "For I will take you from among the nations, gather you out of all countries, and bring you into your own land. Then I will sprinkle clean water on you, and you shall be clean; I will cleanse you from all your filthiness and from all your idols. I will give you a new heart and put a new spirit within you; I will take the heart of stone out of your flesh and give you a heart of flesh. I will put My Spirit within you and cause you to walk in My statutes, and you will keep My judgments and do them" (Ezek. 36:24–27 NKJV).

Under Old Testament law, the Jews could cleanse that which was defiled by using water, fire, or blood. The priests were washed with water and sprinkled with blood when they were installed in office (Lev. 8—9), and the healed lepers were likewise washed with water and sprinkled with blood

(Lev. 14). The priests had to wash their hands and feet and keep ceremonially clean as they served in the tabernacle (Ex. 30:17–21). If anything became defiled, it had to be purified with "the water of sprinkling" (Num. 19). Zechariah used this Old Testament truth to teach about the permanent internal cleansing that would come when the people saw their Messiah and trusted Him (Zech. 12:10). They would experience a new birth and become a new people for the Lord.

A glorious King (v. 21b). What a wonderful way to close a book: "The Lord dwells in Zion!" (NIV). The prophet Ezekiel watched as the glory of God departed from the temple that was about to be destroyed (Ezek. 8:4; 9:3; 10:4, 18; 11:23), and then he saw that glory return to the new temple in the restored nation (43:1–5). He saw a new Jerusalem that had been given a new name: "Jehovah Shammah—the Lord is there" (48:30–35).

The prophecy of Joel begins with tragedy, the invasion of the locusts, but it closes with triumph, the reign of the King of Kings and Lord of Lords. Jesus said to His disciples, "Assuredly I say to you, that in the regeneration [the future kingdom], when the Son of Man sits on the throne of His glory, you who have followed Me will also sit on twelve thrones, judging [ruling over] the twelve tribes of Israel" (Matt. 19:28 NKJV).

May we never lose the wonder of His glorious kingdom!

"The kingdom of the world has become the kingdom of our Lord and of his Christ, and he will reign for ever and ever" (Rev. 11:15 NIV).

"Thy kingdom come" (Matt. 6:10)!

"Even so, come, Lord Jesus" (Rev. 22:20)!

QUESTIONS FOR PERSONAL REFLECTION OR GROUP DISCUSSION

1. Do you think present wars, earthquakes, and famines are "day of the Lord" judgments in God's plan? Explain.

2. Does Joel 2:28–32 speak of the time only right at the very end, the whole "last days" period between the ministry of Christ on earth and the end judgment, or some other time span? What leads you to that conclusion?

3. It seems that the New Testament apostles believed the end was very near in their lifetime. Were they wrong about their urgency? What is a proper attitude about the "when" of the end?

4. Some people believe that the actual "last days" are here. Have you observed, read about, or had any experience that might indicate that we really are at the end? Explain.

5. How can we prepare for the end times?

6. How might theology about the end times differ for people living in areas which have for many years been places of violence, terror, and unrest?

7. Compare the Holy Spirit's role in the Old Testament, in the New Testament, and in your experience. What are the similarities and differences?

8. Wiersbe notes that God uses the possessive pronoun *My* when referring to the Jews, land, and wealth. In what ways do you acknowledge that your money, home, car, kids, spouse, time, and so on belong to God?

9. Wiersbe states that the prophecy of Joel "begins with tragedy … but it closes with triumph." How does this summary help you when you think of things to come?

10. When you look forward to the future kingdom, what is most appealing to you?

JONAH IN HIS TIME

Those who consider the book of Jonah an allegory or a parable should note that 2 Kings 14:25 identifies Jonah as a real person, a Jewish prophet from Gath Hepher in Zebulun who ministered in the northern kingdom of Israel during the reign of Jeroboam II (793–753 BC). They should also note that our Lord considered Jonah a historic person and pointed to him as a type of His own death, burial, and resurrection (Matt. 12:41; Luke 11:32).

The reign of Jeroboam II was a time of great prosperity in Israel; the nation regained lost territory and expanded both its boundaries and influence. But it was a time of moral and spiritual decay as the nation rapidly moved away from God and into idolatry. Jonah's contemporaries Hosea and Amos both courageously denounced the wickedness of the rulers, priests, and people. It's worth noting that Hosea and Amos also showed God's concern for other nations, which is one of the major themes of Jonah.

While Jonah had a ministry to Nineveh, a leading city in Assyria, he also had a ministry to Israel through this little book. He discovered God's compassion for those outside Israel, even those who were their enemies. God had called His people to be a blessing to the Gentiles (Gen. 12:1–3), but, like Jonah, the Jews refused to obey. And, like Jonah, they had to be disciplined; for Assyria would conquer Israel, and Babylon would take Judah into captivity. Jonah's book magnifies the sovereignty of God as well as the love and mercy of God. Jehovah is the "God of the second chance," even for rebellious prophets!

A Suggested Outline of the Book of Jonah

Theme: Obeying God's will brings blessings to us and to others through us; disobedience brings discipline.

Key verse: Jonah 2:9

I. God's Patience with Jonah (Jonah 1:1–17)
1. Jonah's disobedience (Jonah 1:1–3)
2. Jonah's indifference (Jonah 1:4–10)
3. Jonah's impenitence (Jonah 1:11–17)

II. God's Mercy toward Jonah (Jonah 2:1–10)
1. He hears his prayer (Jonah 2:1–2)
2. He disciplines him (Jonah 2:3)
3. He honors his faith (Jonah 2:4–7)
4. He accepts his confession (Jonah 2:8–9)
5. He restores his ministry (Jonah 2:10)

III. God's Power through Jonah (Jonah 3:1–10)
1. The gracious Lord (Jonah 3:1–2)
2. The obedient servant (Jonah 3:3–4)
3. The repentant people (Jonah 3:5–9)
4. The postponed judgment (Jonah 3:10)

IV. God's Ministry to Jonah (Jonah 4:1–11)
1. God hears him (Jonah 4:1–4)
2. God comforts him (Jonah 4:5–8)
3. God teaches him (Jonah 4:9–11)

Chapter Six

PATIENCE AND PARDON

(Jonah 1—2)

Most people are so familiar with the story of Jonah that nothing in it surprises them anymore, including the fact that it begins with the word *and*.¹ If I opened one of my books with the word *and*, the editor would probably wonder if something had been lost, including my ability to use the English language.

Jonah is one of fourteen Old Testament books that open with the little word *and*. These books remind us of God's continued story of grace and mercy. Though the Bible is comprised of sixty-six different books, it tells only one story; and God keeps communicating that message to us, even though we don't always listen too attentively. How long-suffering He is toward us!

What is the book of Jonah about? Well, it's not simply about a great fish (mentioned only four times), or a great city (named nine times), or even a disobedient prophet (mentioned eighteen times). It's about God! God is mentioned thirty-eight times in these four short chapters, and if you eliminated Him from the book, the story wouldn't make sense. The book of Jonah is about the will of God and how we respond to it. It's also about the love of God and how we share it with others.

In these first two chapters, Jonah has three experiences.

1. Rebellion (1:1–17)

Jonah must have been a popular man in Israel, because his prediction had been fulfilled that the nation would regain her lost territory from her enemies (2 Kings 14:25). Those were days of peace and prosperity for Israel, but they were autumn days just before the terrible winter of judgment.

Jonah the prophet disobeys God's call (vv. 1–3). Jonah got into trouble because his attitudes were wrong. To begin with, he had a wrong attitude toward the will of God. Obeying the will of God is as important to God's servant as it is to the people His servants minister to. It's in obeying the will of God that we find our spiritual nourishment (John 4:34), enlightenment (7:17), and enablement (Heb. 13:21). To Jesus, the will of God was food that satisfied Him; to Jonah, the will of God was medicine that choked him.

Jonah's wrong attitude toward God's will stemmed from a feeling that the Lord was asking him to do an impossible thing. God commanded the prophet to go to Israel's enemy, Assyria, and give the city of Nineveh opportunity to repent, and Jonah would much rather see the city destroyed. The Assyrians were a cruel people who had often abused Israel, and Jonah's narrow patriotism took precedence over his theology.[2] Jonah forgot that the will of God is the expression of the love of God (Ps. 33:11), and that God called him to Nineveh because He loved both Jonah and the Ninevites.

Jonah also had a wrong attitude toward the Word of God. When the Word of the Lord came to him, Jonah thought he could "take it or leave it." However, when God's Word commands us, we must listen and obey. Disobedience isn't an option. "But why do you call Me 'Lord, Lord,' and not do the things which I say?" (Luke 6:46 NKJV).

Jonah forgot that it was a great privilege to be a prophet, to hear God's Word, and know God's will. That's why he resigned his prophetic office and fled in the opposite direction from Nineveh.[3] Jonah knew that he couldn't run away from God's presence (Ps. 139:7–12), but he felt he had the right to turn in his resignation. He forgot that "God's gifts and his call are irrevocable" (Rom. 11:29 NIV). At one time or another during their ministries, Moses, Elijah, and Jeremiah felt like giving up, but God wouldn't let them. Jonah needed Nineveh as much as Nineveh needed Jonah. It's in doing the will of God that we grow in grace and become more like Christ.

Jonah had a wrong attitude toward circumstances; he thought they were working for him when they were really working against him. He fled to Joppa[4] and found just the right ship waiting for him! He had enough money to pay the fare for his long trip, and he was even able to go down into the ship and fall into a sleep so deep that the storm didn't wake him up. It's possible to be out of the will of God and still have circumstances appear to be working on your behalf. You can be rebelling against God and still have a false sense of security that includes a good night's sleep. God in His providence was preparing Jonah for a great fall.

Finally, Jonah had a wrong attitude toward the Gentiles. Instead of wanting to help them find the true and living God, he wanted to abandon them to their darkness and spiritual death. He not only hated their sins—and the Assyrians were ruthless enemies—but he hated the sinners who committed the sins. Better that Nineveh should be destroyed than the Assyrians live and attack Israel.

Jonah the Jew becomes a curse instead of a blessing (vv. 4–10). God called the Jews to be a blessing to all the nations of the earth (Gen. 12:1–3), but whenever the Jews were out of the will of God, they brought trouble instead of blessing.[5] Twice Abraham brought trouble to people because he lied (vv. 10–20; 20:1–18); Achan brought trouble to Israel's army because he robbed God (Josh. 7); and Jonah brought trouble to a boatload of pagan sailors because he fled. Consider all that Jonah lost because he wasn't a blessing to others.

First of all, he *lost the voice of God (Jonah 1:4)*. We don't read that "the

Word of the Lord came to Jonah," but that a great storm broke loose over the waters. God was no longer speaking to Jonah through His Word; He was speaking to him through His works: the sea, the wind, the rain, the thunder, and even the great fish. Everything in nature obeyed God except His servant! God even spoke to Jonah through the heathen sailors (vv. 6, 8, 10) who didn't know Jehovah. It's a sad thing when a servant of God is rebuked by pagans.

Jonah also *lost his spiritual energy (v. 5b)*. He went to sleep during a fierce storm and was totally unconcerned about the safety of others. The sailors were throwing the ship's wares and cargo overboard, and Jonah was about to lose everything, but he still slept on. "A little sleep, a little slumber, a little folding of the hands to rest—and poverty will come on you like a bandit and scarcity like an armed man" (Prov. 24:33 NIV).

He *lost his power in prayer (Jonah 1:5a, 6)*. The heathen sailors were calling on their gods for help while Jonah slept through the prayer meeting, the one man on board who knew the true God and could pray to Him. Of course, Jonah would first have had to confess his sins and determine to obey God, something he wasn't willing to do. "If I regard iniquity in my heart, the Lord will not hear me" (Ps. 66:18).[6] If Jonah did pray, his prayer wasn't answered. Loss of power in prayer is one of the first indications that we're far from the Lord and need to get right with Him.

Sad to say, Jonah *lost his testimony (Jonah 1:7–10)*. He certainly wasn't living up to his name,[7] for Jonah means "dove," and the dove is a symbol of peace. Jonah's father's name was Ammitai, which means "faithful, truthful," something that Jonah was not. We've already seen that he wasn't living up to his high calling as a Jew, for he had brought everybody trouble instead of blessing, nor was he living up to his calling as a prophet, for he had no message for them from God. When the lot pointed to Jonah as the culprit, he could no longer avoid making a decision.

Jonah had already told the crew that he was running away from God, but now he told them he was God's prophet, the God who created the heaven, the earth, and the sea. This announcement made the sailors even more frightened. The God who created the sea was punishing His servant and that's why they were in danger!

Jonah the rebel suffers for his sins (vv. 11–17). Charles Spurgeon said that God never allows His children to sin successfully, and Jonah is proof of the truth of that statement. "For whom the Lord loves He chastens, and scourges every son whom He receives" (Heb. 12:6 NKJV).

We must not make the mistake of calling Jonah a martyr, for the title would be undeserved. Martyrs die for the glory of God, but Jonah offered to die because selfishly he would rather die than obey the will of God![8] He shouldn't be classified with people like Moses (Ex. 32:30–35), Esther (Est. 4:13–17), and Paul (Rom. 9:1–3), who were willing to give their lives to God in order to rescue others. Jonah is to be commended for telling the truth but not for taking his life in his own hands. He should have surrendered his life to the Lord and let Him give the orders. Had he fallen to his knees and confessed his sins to God, Jonah might have seen the storm cease and the door open to a great opportunity for witness on the ship.

It's significant that the heathen sailors at first rejected Jonah's offer and began to work harder to save the ship. They did more for Jonah than Jonah had been willing to do for them. When they saw that the cause was hopeless, they asked Jonah's God for His forgiveness for throwing Jonah into the stormy sea. Sometimes unsaved people put believers to shame by their honesty, sympathy, and sacrifice.

However, these pagan sailors knew some basic theology: the existence of Jonah's God, His judgment of sin, their own guilt before Him, and His sovereignty over creation. They confessed, "For you, O Lord, have done as you pleased" (Jonah 1:14 NIV). However, there's no evidence that they abandoned their old gods; they merely added Jehovah to their "god shelf."

They threw themselves on God's mercy and then threw Jonah into the raging sea, and God stopped the storm.

When the storm ceased, the men feared God even more and made vows to Him. How they could offer an animal sacrifice to God on board ship is a puzzle to us, especially since the cargo had been jettisoned, but then we don't know what the sacrifice was or how it was offered. Perhaps the sense of verse 16 is that they offered the animal to Jehovah and vowed to sacrifice it to Him once they were safe on shore.

The seventeenth-century English preacher Jeremy Taylor said, "God threatens terrible things if we will not be happy." He was referring, of course, to being happy with God's will for our lives. For us to rebel against God's will, as Jonah did, is to invite the chastening hand of God. That's why the Westminster Catechism states that "the chief end of man is to glorify God and enjoy Him forever." We glorify God by enjoying His will and doing it from our hearts (Eph. 6:6), and that's where Jonah failed.

Jonah could say with the psalmist, "The Lord has chastened me severely, but He has not given me over to death" (Ps. 118:18 NKJV). God prepared a great fish to swallow Jonah and protect his life for three days and three nights.[9] We'll consider the significance of this later in this study.

2. REPENTANCE (2:1–9)

From an experience of rebellion and discipline, Jonah turns to an experience of repentance and dedication, and God graciously gives him a new beginning. Jonah no doubt expected to die in the waters of the sea,[10] but when he woke up inside the fish, he realized that God had graciously spared him. As with the Prodigal Son, whom Jonah in his rebellion greatly resembles (Luke 15:11–24), it was the goodness of God that brought him to repentance (Rom. 2:4). Notice the stages in Jonah's spiritual experience as described in his prayer.

He prayed for God's help (vv. 1–2). "Then Jonah prayed" (2:1) suggests that it was at the end of the three days and three nights when Jonah turned to the Lord for help, but we probably shouldn't press the word *then* too far. The Hebrew text simply reads, "And Jonah prayed." Surely Jonah prayed as he went down into the depths of the sea, certain that he would drown. That would be the normal thing for any person to do, and that's the picture we get from verses 5 and 7.

His prayer was born out of affliction, not affection. He cried out to God because he was in danger, not because he delighted in the Lord. But better that he should pray compelled by any motive than not to pray at all. It's doubtful whether any believer always prays with pure and holy motives, for our desires and God's directions sometimes conflict.

However, in spite of the fact that he prayed, Jonah still wasn't happy with the will of God. In chapter 1, he was afraid of the will of God and rebelled against it, but now he wants God's will simply because it's the only way out of his dangerous plight. Like too many people today, Jonah saw the will of God as something to turn to in an emergency, not something to live by every day of one's life.

Jonah was now experiencing what the sailors experienced during the storm: He felt he was perishing (1:6, 14). It's good for God's people, and especially preachers, to remember what it's like to be lost and without hope. How easy it is for us to grow hardened toward sinners and lose our compassion for the lost. As He dropped Jonah into the depths, God was reminding him of what the people of Nineveh were going through in their sinful condition: They were helpless and hopeless.

God heard Jonah's cries for help. Prayer is one of the constant miracles of the Christian life. To think that our God is so great He can hear the cries of millions of people at the same time and deal with their needs personally! A parent with two or three children often finds it impossible to meet all their needs all the time, but God is able to provide for all His children, no matter where they are or what their needs may be. "He who has learned to pray," said William Law, "has learned the greatest secret of a holy and happy life."

He accepted God's discipline (v. 3). The sailors didn't cast Jonah into the stormy sea; God did. "*You* hurled me into the deep ... all *your* waves and breakers swept over me" (v. 3 NIV). When Jonah said those words, he was acknowledging that God was disciplining him and that he deserved it.

How we respond to discipline determines how much benefit we receive from it. According to Hebrews 12:5–11, we have several options: We can despise God's discipline and fight (v. 5); we can be discouraged and faint (v. 5); we can resist discipline and invite stronger discipline, possibly even death (v. 9);[11] or we can submit to the Father and mature in faith and love (v. 7). Discipline is to the believer what exercise and training are to the athlete (v. 11); it enables us to run the race with endurance and reach the assigned goal (vv. 1–2).

The fact that God chastened His servant is proof that Jonah was truly a child of God, for God disciplines only His own children. "But if you are without chastening, of which all have become partakers, then you are illegitimate and not sons" (v. 8 NKJV). And the father chastens us in love so that "afterward" we might enjoy "the peaceable fruit of righteousness" (v. 11).

He trusted God's promises (vv. 4–7). Jonah was going in one direction only—down. In fact, he had been going in that direction since the hour he rebelled against God's plan for his life. He went "down to Joppa" and "down into the sides of the ship" (1:3, 5). Now he was going "down to the bottoms of the mountains" (2:6); and at some point, the great fish met him, and he went down into the fish's belly (1:17). When you turn your back on God, the only direction you can go is down.

What saved Jonah? His faith in God's promise. Which promise? The promise that involves "looking toward God's holy temple" (2:4, 7). When

King Solomon dedicated the temple in Jerusalem, he asked God for this special favor (1 Kings 8:38–40 NKJV):

> Whatever prayer, whatever supplication is made by anyone, or by all Your people Israel, when each one knows the plague of his own heart, and spreads out his hands toward this temple: then hear in heaven Your dwelling place, and forgive, and act, and give to everyone according to all his ways, whose heart You know … that they may fear You all the days that they live in the land which You gave to our fathers.

Jonah claimed that promise. By faith, he looked toward God's temple (the only way to look was up!) and asked God to deliver him; and God kept His promise and answered his call. "I remembered [the] Lord" (Jonah 2:7) means, "I acted on the basis of His commitment to me." Jonah knew God's covenant promises, and he claimed them.

He yielded to God's will (vv. 8–9). Now Jonah admits that there were idols in his life that robbed him of the blessing of God. An idol is anything that takes away from God the affection and obedience that rightfully belong only to Him. One such idol was Jonah's intense patriotism. He was so concerned for the safety and prosperity of his own nation that he refused to be God's messenger to their enemies the Assyrians. We shall learn from chapter 4 that Jonah was also protecting his own reputation (4:2), for if God spared Nineveh, then Jonah would be branded a false prophet whose words of warning weren't fulfilled. For somebody who was famous for his prophecies (2 Kings 14:25), this would be devastating.

Jonah closes his prayer by uttering some solemn vows to the Lord, vows that he really intended to keep. Like the psalmist, he said, "I will go into Your house with burnt offerings; I will pay You my vows, which my lips have uttered and my mouth has spoken when I was in trouble" (Ps. 66:13–14 NKJV). Jonah promised to worship God in the temple with sacrifices and songs of thanksgiving. He doesn't tell us what other promises he made to the Lord, but one of them surely was, "I will go to Nineveh and declare Your message if You give me another chance."

Jonah couldn't save himself, and nobody on earth could save him, but the Lord could do it, for "salvation is of the LORD" (Jonah 2:9 NKJV)! This is a quotation from Psalms 3:8 and 37:39, and it is the central declaration in the book. It is also the central theme of the Bible. How wise of Jonah to memorize the Word of God; because being able to quote the Scriptures, especially the book of Psalms, gave him light in the darkness and hope in his seemingly hopeless situation.

3. REDEMPTION (2:10)

"And [the fish] vomited out Jonah upon the dry land." What an ignominious way for a distinguished prophet to arrive on shore! In chapter 1, the sailors treated Jonah like dangerous cargo to be thrown overboard, and now he's treated like a foreign substance to be disgorged from the fish's body. But when Jonah ceased to be an obedient prophet, he cheapened himself, so he's the one to blame. We can be sure that he was duly humbled as he once again stood on dry land.

The miracle. Few miracles in Scripture have been attacked as much as this one, and Christian scholars have gathered various kinds of evidence to prove that it could happen. Since the Bible doesn't tell us what kind of fish swallowed Jonah, we don't have to measure sharks and whales or comb history for similar incidents. It was a "prepared" fish (1:17), designed by God for the occasion, and therefore it was adequate for the task. Jesus didn't question the historicity of the miracle, so why should we?

The sign (Matt. 12:39; 16:4; Luke 11:29). The "sign of Jonah" is seen in his experience of "death," burial, and resurrection on the third day, and it was the only sign Jesus gave to the nation of Israel. At Pentecost, Peter preached the resurrection (Acts 2:22–26) and so did Paul when he preached to the Jews in other nations (13:26–37). In fact, the emphasis in the book of Acts is on the resurrection of Jesus Christ; for the apostles were "witnesses" of the resurrection (2:32; 3:15; 5:32; 10:39).

Some students are troubled by the phrase "three days and three nights," especially since both Scripture and tradition indicate that Jesus was crucified on Friday. In order to protect the integrity of the Scripture, some have suggested that the crucifixion be moved back to Thursday or even Wednesday. But to the Jews, a part of a day was treated as a whole day, and we need not interpret "three days and three nights" to mean seventy-two hours to the very second. For that matter, we can't prove that Jonah was in the fish exactly seventy-two hours. The important thing is that centuries after the event, Jonah became a "sign" to the Jewish people and pointed them to Jesus Christ.

Jonah was now free to obey the Lord and take God's message to Nineveh, but he still had lessons to learn.

QUESTIONS FOR PERSONAL REFLECTION
OR GROUP DISCUSSION

1. Wiersbe writes that the beginning word *and* in the book of Jonah "reminds us of God's continued story of grace and mercy." How would your thoughts about your place in God's plan be changed if you thought of your story as being linked to Bible times and church history with the word *and*?

2. How did Jonah experience rebellion? Repentance? Redemption? How does this compare with the salvation each of us experiences?

3. What three things did Jonah have a bad attitude about? What was bad about his attitude toward each of these?

4. Have you ever had a wrong attitude about God's will because you thought what God wanted was impossible? If so, what was the thing that seemed impossible to you?

5. One of Jonah's problems was that his "narrow patriotism took precedence over his theology." In what ways are Christians in your country vulnerable to "narrow patriotism"? What would appropriate patriotism involve?

6. Jonah seemed to have a "take it or leave it" attitude toward the Word of the Lord. Which portions of the Word of God (particular passages or topics) have you been tempted to discard?

7. At what point in your life were you closest to turning in your resignation to God? Why?

8. What four things did Jonah lose because he wasn't a blessing to others and was disobedient? Choose one of these, and talk about a time when you lost that because you weren't being a blessing to others.

9. How do you think God views your struggle with mixed motives in your prayers?

10. What can help us to remember what it is like to be lost and without hope?

11. Wiersbe writes, "Jonah couldn't save himself, and nobody on earth could save him, but the Lord could do it, for 'salvation is of the LORD' (Jonah 2:9 NKJV)." How is this truth important in your life?

PREACHING AND POUTING

(Jonah 3—4)

The question is usually asked in Old Testament survey classes, "Was the great fish more relieved to be rid of Jonah than Jonah was to get out of the great fish?" Maybe their sense of relief was mutual. At any rate, we hope that Jonah gave thanks to God for the divinely provided creature that rescued him from certain death.

In these two chapters, we are confronted with four marvels that we dare not take for granted.

1. THE MARVEL OF AN UNDESERVED COMMISSION (3:1–2)

Did anybody see Jonah emerge when the great fish disgorged him on the dry land? If so, the story must have spread rapidly and perhaps even preceded him to Nineveh, and that may help explain the reception the city gave him. Had Jonah been bleached by the fish's gastric juices? Did he look so peculiar that nobody could doubt who he was and what had happened to him? Since Jonah was a "sign" to the Ninevites (Matt. 12:38–41), perhaps this included the way he looked.

What the people saw or thought really wasn't important. The important thing was what God thought and what He would do next to His repentant prophet. "The life of Jonah cannot be written without God," said Charles Spurgeon; "take God out of the prophet's history, and there is no history to write."[1]

God met Jonah. We don't know where the great fish deposited Jonah, but we do know that wherever Jonah was, the Lord was there. Remember, God is more concerned about His workers than He is about their work, for if the workers are what they ought to be, the work will be what it ought to be. Throughout Jonah's time of rebellion, God was displeased with His servant, but He never once deserted him. It was God who controlled the storm, prepared the great fish, and rescued Jonah from the deep. His promise is, "I will never leave you nor forsake you" (Heb. 13:5 NKJV; see Josh. 1:5). "When you pass through the waters, I will be with you" (Isa. 43:2 NKJV).

God spoke to Jonah. After the way Jonah had stubbornly refused to obey God's voice, it's a marvel that the Lord spoke to him at all. Jonah had turned his back on God's Word, so the Lord had been forced to speak to him through thunder and rain and a stormy sea. But now that Jonah had confessed his sins and turned back to the Lord, God could once again speak to him through His Word. One of the tests of our relationship to God is, "Does God speak to me as I read and ponder His Word?" If we don't hear God speaking to us in our hearts, perhaps we have some unfinished business that needs to be settled with Him.

God commissioned Jonah. One of the most beautiful aspects of the Christian faith is the element of renewal. When we fall, the enemy wants us to believe that our ministry is ended and there's no hope for recovery, but our God is the God of the second chance. "Then the word of the Lord came to Jonah a second time" (Jonah 3:1 NIV). "Do not rejoice over me, my enemy; when I fall, I will arise; when I sit in darkness, the Lord will be a light to me" (Mic. 7:8 NKJV).

You don't have to read very far in your Bible to discover that God forgives His servants and restores them to ministry. Abraham fled to Egypt, where he lied about his wife, but God gave him another chance (Gen. 12:10—13:4). Jacob lied to his father, Isaac, but God restored him and used him to build the nation of Israel. Moses killed a man (probably in self-defense) and fled from Egypt, but God called him to be the leader of His people. Peter denied the Lord three times, but Jesus forgave him and said, "Follow me" (John 21:19).

However encouraging these examples of restoration may be, they must never be used as excuses for sin. The person who says, "I can go ahead and sin, because I know the Lord will forgive me" has no understanding of the awfulness of sin or the holiness of God. "But there is forgiveness with You, that You may be feared" (Ps. 130:4 NKJV). God in His grace forgives our sins, but God in His government determines that we shall reap what we sow, and the harvest can be very costly. Jonah paid dearly for rebelling against the Lord.

God challenged Jonah. Four times in this book, Nineveh is called a "great city" (1:2; 3:2–3; 4:11),[2] and archeologists tell us that the adjective is well deserved. It was great in history, having been founded in ancient times by Noah's great-grandson Nimrod (Gen. 10:8–10).[3] It was also great in size. The circumference of the city and its suburbs was sixty miles, and from the Lord's statement in Jonah 4:11, we could infer that there were probably over six hundred thousand people living there. One wall of the city had a circumference of eight miles and boasted fifteen hundred towers.

The city was great in splendor and influence, being one of the leading cities of the powerful Assyrian Empire. It was built near the Tigris River and had the Khoser River running through it. (This fact will prove to be important when we study the book of Nahum.) Its merchants traveled the empire and brought great wealth into the city, and Assyria's armies were feared everywhere.

Nineveh was great in sin, for the Assyrians were known far and wide for their violence, showing no mercy to their enemies. They impaled live victims on sharp poles, leaving them to roast to death in the desert sun; they beheaded people by the thousands and stacked their skulls up in piles by the city gates; and they even skinned people alive. They respected neither age nor sex and followed a policy of killing babies and young children so they wouldn't have to care for them (Nah. 3:10).

It was to the wicked people of this great city that God sent His servant Jonah, assuring him that He would give him the message to speak. After making the necessary preparations, it would take Jonah at least a month to travel from his own land to the city of Nineveh, and during that trip, he had a lot of time available to meditate on what the Lord had taught him.

The will of God will never lead you where the grace of God can't keep you and the power of God can't use you. "And who is sufficient for these things? … Our sufficiency is of God" (2 Cor. 2:16; 3:5).

2. The Marvel of an Unparalleled Awakening (3:3–10)

From a human perspective, this entire enterprise appears ridiculous. How could one man, claiming to be God's prophet, confront thousands of people with this strange message, especially a message of judgment? How could a Jew, who worshipped the true God, ever get these idolatrous Gentiles to believe what he had to say? For all he knew, Jonah might end up impaled on a pole or skinned alive! But, in obedience to the Lord, Jonah went to Nineveh.

Jonah's message to Nineveh (vv. 3–4). "Three days' journey" means either that it would take three days to get through the city and its suburbs or three days to go around them. The NIV translation of verse 3 suggests that it would take three days to visit all of the area. According to Genesis 10:11–12, four cities were involved in the "Nineveh metroplex": Nineveh, Rehoboth Ir, Calah, and Resen (NIV). However you interpret the "three days," one thing is clear: Nineveh was no insignificant place.

When Jonah was one day into the city, he began to declare his message: "Yet forty days, and Nineveh shall be overthrown." Throughout Scripture, the number forty seems to be identified with testing or judgment. During the time of Noah, it rained forty days and forty nights (Gen. 7:4, 12, 17). The Jewish spies explored Canaan forty days (Num. 14:34), and the nation of Israel was tested in the wilderness forty years (Deut. 2:7). The giant Goliath taunted the army of Israel forty days (1 Sam. 17:16), and the Lord gave the people of Nineveh forty days to repent and turn from their wickedness.

At this point, we must confess that we wish we knew more about Jonah's ministry to Nineveh. Was this the only message he proclaimed? Surely he spent time telling the people about the true and living God, for we're told, "The people of Nineveh believed God" (Jonah 3:5). They would have to know something about this God of Israel in order to exercise sincere faith (see Acts 17:22ff.). Did Jonah expose the folly of their idolatry? Did he recount his own personal history to show them that his God was powerful and sovereign? We simply don't know. The important thing is that Jonah obeyed God, went to Nineveh, and declared the message God gave him. God did the rest.

Nineveh's message to God (vv. 5–9). In the Hebrew text, there are only five words in Jonah's message; yet God used those five words to stir the entire population, from the king on the throne to the lowest peasant in the field. God gave the people forty days of grace, but they didn't need that long. We get the impression that from the very first time they saw Jonah and heard his warning, they paid attention to his message. Word spread quickly throughout the entire district, and the people humbled themselves by fasting and wearing sackcloth.

When the message got to the king, he too put on sackcloth and sat in the dust. He also made the fast official by issuing an edict and ordering the people to humble themselves, cry out to God, and turn from their evil ways. Even the animals were included in the activities by wearing sackcloth and abstaining from food and drink. The people were to cry "mightily" ("urgently" NIV) to God, for this was a matter of life and death (Jonah 3:8).

When Jonah was in dire straits, he recalled the promise concerning Solomon's temple (Jonah 2:4, 7; 1 Kings 8:38–39; 2 Chron. 6:36–39), looking toward the temple, and called out for help. Included in Solomon's temple prayer was a promise for people outside the nation of Israel, and that would include the Ninevites. "As for the foreigner who does not belong to your people Israel ... when he comes and prays toward this temple, then hear from heaven, your dwelling place, and do whatever the foreigner asks of you, so that all the peoples of the earth may know your name and fear you" (2 Chron. 6:32–33 NIV). Jonah certainly knew this promise, and perhaps it was the basis for the whole awakening.

Like the sailors in the storm, the Ninevites didn't want to perish (Jonah 3:9; 1:6, 14). That's what witnessing is all about, "that whoever believes in Him should not perish but have everlasting life" (John 3:16 NKJV). Their fasting and praying, and their humbling of themselves before God, sent a message to heaven, but the people of Nineveh had no assurance that they would be saved. They hoped that God's great compassion would move Him to change His plan and spare the city. Once again, how did they know that the God of the Hebrews was a merciful and compassionate God? No doubt Jonah told them, for this was a doctrine he himself believed (Jonah 4:2).

God's message (v. 10). At some point, God spoke to Jonah and told him that He had accepted the people's repentance and would not destroy the city. The phrase "God repented" might better be translated "God relented," that is, changed His course. From the human point of view, it looked like repentance, but from the divine perspective, it was simply God's response to man's change of heart. God is utterly consistent with Himself; it only appears that He is changing His mind. The Bible uses human analogies to reveal the divine character of God (Jer. 18:1–10).

How deep was the spiritual experience of the people of Nineveh? If repentance and faith are the basic conditions of salvation (Acts 20:21), then we have reason to believe that they were accepted by God; for the people of Nineveh repented and had faith in God (Jonah 3:5). The fact that Jesus used the Ninevites to shame the unbelieving Jews of His day is further evidence that their response to Jonah's ministry was sincere (Matt. 12:38–41).

3. THE MARVEL OF AN UNHAPPY SERVANT (4:1–11)

If this book had ended at the last verse of chapter 3, history would have portrayed Jonah as the greatest of the prophets. After all, preaching one message that motivated thousands of people to repent and turn to God was no mean accomplishment. But the Lord doesn't look on the outward things; He looks at the heart (1 Sam. 16:7) and weighs the motives (1 Cor. 4:5). That's why chapter 4 was included in the book, for it reveals "the thoughts and intents" of Jonah's heart and exposes his sins.

If in chapter 1 Jonah is like the Prodigal Son, insisting on doing his own thing and going his own way (Luke 15:11–32); then in chapter 4, he's like the Prodigal's elder brother—critical, selfish, sullen, angry, and unhappy with what was going on. It isn't enough for God's servants simply to do their Master's will; they must do "the will of God from the heart" (Eph. 6:6). The heart of every problem is the problem in the heart, and that's where Jonah's problems were to be found. "But it displeased Jonah exceedingly, and he was very angry" (Jonah 4:1).

The remarkable thing is that God tenderly dealt with His sulking servant and sought to bring him back to the place of joy and fellowship.

God listened to Jonah (vv. 1–4). For the second time in this account, Jonah prayed, but his second prayer was much different in content and intent. He prayed his best prayer in the worst place, the fish's belly, and he prayed his worst prayer in the best place, at Nineveh where God was working. His first prayer came from a broken heart, but his second prayer came from an angry heart. In his first prayer, he asked God to save him, but in his second prayer, he asked God to take his life! Once again, Jonah would rather die than not have his own way.

This petulant prayer lets us in on the secret of why Jonah tried to run away in the first place. Being a good theologian, Jonah knew the attributes of God, that He was "a gracious and compassionate God, slow to anger and abounding in love, a God who relents from sending calamity" (Jonah 4:2 NIV). Knowing this, Jonah was sure that if he announced judgment to the Ninevites and they repented, God would forgive them and not send His judgment, and then Jonah would be branded as a false prophet! Remember, Jonah's message merely announced the impending judgment; it didn't offer conditions for salvation.

Jonah was concerned about his reputation, not only before the Ninevites, but also before the Jews back home. His Jewish friends would want to see all of the Assyrians destroyed, not just the people of Nineveh. When Jonah's friends found out that he had been the means of saving Nineveh from God's wrath, they could have considered him a traitor to official Jewish foreign policy. Jonah was a narrow-minded patriot who saw Assyria only as a dangerous enemy to destroy, not as a company of repentant sinners to be brought to the Lord.

When reputation is more important than character, and pleasing ourselves and our friends is more important than pleasing God, then we're in danger of becoming like Jonah and living to defend our prejudices instead of fulfilling our spiritual responsibilities.[4] Jonah certainly had good theology, but it stayed in his head and never got to his heart, and he was so distraught that he wanted to die![5] God's tender response was to ask Jonah to examine his heart and see why he really was angry.

God comforted Jonah (vv. 5–8). For the second time in this book, Jonah abandoned his place of ministry, left the city, and sat down in a place east of the city where he could see what would happen. Like the elder brother in the parable, he wouldn't go in and enjoy the feast (Luke 15:28). He could have taught the Ninevites so much about the true God of Israel, but he preferred to have his own way. What a tragedy it is when God's servants are a means of blessing to others but miss the blessing themselves!

God knew that Jonah was very uncomfortable sitting in that booth, so He graciously caused a vine (gourd) to grow whose large leaves would protect Jonah from the hot sun. This made Jonah happy, but the next morning, when God prepared a worm to kill the vine, Jonah was unhappy. The combination of the hot sun and the smothering desert wind made him want to die even more. As He had done in the depths of the sea, God was reminding Jonah of what it was like to be lost: helpless, hopeless, miserable. Jonah was experiencing a taste of hell as he sat and watched the city.

A simple test of character is to ask, "What makes me happy? What makes me angry? What makes me want to give up?" Jonah was "a double-minded man, unstable in all his ways" (James 1:8 NKJV). One minute he's preaching God's Word, but the next minute he's disobeying it and fleeing his post of duty. While inside the great fish, he prayed to be delivered, but now he asks the Lord to kill him. He called the city to repentance, but he wouldn't repent himself! He was more concerned about creature comforts than he was about winning the lost. The Ninevites, the vine, the worm, and the wind have all obeyed God, but Jonah still refuses to obey, and he has the most to gain.

God instructed Jonah (vv. 9–11). God is still speaking to Jonah and Jonah is still listening and answering, even though he's not giving the right answers. Unrighteous anger feeds the ego and produces the poison of selfishness in the heart. Jonah still had a problem with the will of God. In chapter 1, his mind understood God's will, but he refused to obey it and took his body in the opposite direction. In chapter 2, he cried out for help, God rescued him, and he gave his body back to the Lord. In chapter 3, he yielded his will to the Lord and went to Nineveh to preach, but his heart was not yet surrendered to the Lord. Jonah did the will of God, but not from his heart.

Jonah had one more lesson to learn, perhaps the most important one of all. In chapter 1, he learned the lesson of God's providence and patience, that you can't run away from God. In chapter 2, he learned the lesson of God's pardon, that God forgives those who call upon Him. In chapter 3, he learned the lesson of God's power as he saw a whole city humble itself before the Lord. Now he had to learn the lesson of God's pity, that God has compassion for lost sinners like the Ninevites; and his servants must also have compassion.[6] It seems incredible, but Jonah brought a whole city to faith in the Lord, and yet he didn't love the people he was preaching to!

The people who could not "discern between their right hand and their left hand" (4:11) were immature little children (Deut. 1:39), and if there were 120,000 of them in Nineveh and its suburbs, the population was not small. God certainly has a special concern for the children (Mark 10:13–16); but whether children or adults, the Assyrians all needed to know the Lord. Jonah had pity on the vine that perished, but he didn't have compassion for the people who would perish and live eternally apart from God.

Jeremiah and Jesus looked on the city of Jerusalem and wept over it (Jer. 9:1, 10; 23:9; Luke 19:41), and Paul beheld the city of Athens and "was greatly distressed" (Acts 17:16 NIV), but Jonah looked on the city of Nineveh and seethed with anger. He needed to learn the lesson of God's pity and have a heart of compassion for lost souls.

4. The Marvel of an Unanswered Question (4:11)

Jonah and Nahum are the only books in the Bible that end with questions, and both books have to do with the city of Nineveh. Nahum ends with a question about God's punishment of Nineveh (Nah. 3:19), while Jonah ends with a question about God's pity for Nineveh.

This is a strange way to end such a dramatic book as the book of Jonah. God has the first word (Jonah 1:1–2) and God has the last word (4:11), and that's as it should be, but we aren't told how Jonah answered God's final question. It's like the ending of Frank Stockton's famous short story "The Lady or the Tiger?" When the handsome youth opened the door, what came out: the beautiful princess or the man-eating tiger?

We sincerely hope that Jonah yielded to God's loving entreaty and followed the example of the Ninevites by repenting and seeking the face of God. The famous Scottish preacher Alexander Whyte believed that Jonah did experience a change of heart. He wrote, "But Jonah came to himself again during those five-and-twenty days or so, from the east gate of Nineveh back to Gath Hepher, his father's house."[7] Spurgeon said, "Let us hope that, during the rest of his life, he so lived as to rejoice in the sparing mercy of God."[8] After all, hadn't Jonah himself been spared because of God's mercy?

God was willing to spare Nineveh, but in order to do that, He could not spare His own Son. Somebody had to die for their sins or they would die in their sins. "He that spared not his own Son, but delivered him up for us all, how shall he not with him also freely give us all things?" (Rom. 8:32). Jesus used Jonah's ministry to Nineveh to show the Jews how guilty they were in rejecting His witness. "The men of Nineveh shall rise in judgment with this generation, and shall condemn it; because they repented at the preaching of Jonas [Jonah]; and, behold, a greater than Jonas is here" (Matt. 12:41).

How is Jesus greater than Jonah? Certainly Jesus is greater than Jonah in His person, for though both were Jews and both were prophets, Jesus is the very Son of God. He is greater in His message, for Jonah preached a message of judgment, but Jesus preached a message of grace and salvation (John 3:16–17). Jonah almost died for his own sins, but Jesus willingly died for the sins of the world (1 John 2:2).

Jonah's ministry was to but one city, but Jesus is "the Savior of the world" (John 4:42; 1 John 4:14). Jonah's obedience was not from the heart, but Jesus always did whatever pleased His Father (John 8:29). Jonah didn't love the people he came to save, but Jesus had compassion for sinners and proved His love by dying for them on the cross (Rom. 5:6–8). On the cross, outside the city, Jesus asked God to forgive those who killed Him (Luke 23:34), but Jonah waited outside the city to see if God would kill those he would not forgive.

Yes, Jesus is greater than Jonah, and because He is, we must give greater heed to what He says to us. Those who reject Him will face greater judgment because the greater the light, the greater the responsibility.

But the real issue isn't how Jonah answered God's question; the real issue is how you and I today are answering God's question. Do we agree with God that people without Christ are lost? Like God, do we have compassion for those who are lost? How do we show this compassion? Do we have a concern for those in our great cities where there is so much sin and so little witness? Do we pray that the gospel will go to people in every part of the world, and are we helping to send it there? Do we rejoice when sinners repent and trust the Savior?

All of those questions and more are wrapped up in what God asked Jonah.

We can't answer for him, but we can answer for ourselves.

Let's give God the right answer.

QUESTIONS FOR PERSONAL REFLECTION
OR GROUP DISCUSSION

1. What are the four "marvels" Wiersbe highlights in Jonah 3—4? Which of these is the most amazing to you? Why?

2. God never deserted Jonah, even in Jonah's rebellion. What evidence of this promise-keeping care of God have you personally seen? What comfort is it for your future?

3. When you sin, how do you feel in God's presence? How do you respond to God's new beginning for you: (a) readily accept it and are thankful, (b) tend to take it for granted, (c) feel guilty, or (d) can't really believe it but want to. Explain.

4. Like preaching to the wicked Ninevites, what ministry situations look ridiculous or impossible to you from your human perspective?

5. How did these violent Ninevites turn so easily and quickly to the Lord?

6. Jonah 3:10 says God "repented" or "relented" (NASB). Where else in Scripture do you find God repenting/relenting/changing His mind? How does this fit with God's sovereignty?

7. Is there anybody toward whom you have a bad attitude, as Jonah did? How does it affect you to think of God using you for good in that person's (or those people's) life?

8. How real is God's tenderness to you? How can we reflect that tenderness in our dealings with others?

9. In what situations have you had to struggle with wanting people to like and respect you more than you wanted to please God and exhibit godly character?

10. Jonah learned about God's providence and patience (chapter 1), that you can't run away from God. He learned about God's pardon (chapter 2), that God forgives those who call upon Him. He learned of God's power (chapter 3) as he saw a whole city humble itself before the Lord. Then he learned of God's pity (chapter 4), that God has compassion for lost sinners like the Ninevites; and His servants must also have compassion. Which of these lessons is God's priority for you today?

NAHUM IN HIS TIME

Little is known about Nahum except that he came from the town of Elkosh, whose location we can't identify with certainty, and that he was a prophet of God who announced the fall of Nineveh, capital city of the Assyrian Empire. He mentions the capture of the Egyptian city of Thebes (No-Ammon, 3:8–10), which occurred in 663 BC, and he predicted the fall of Nineveh, which took place in 612 BC; so these dates place him in Judah during the reigns of Manasseh (695–642) and Josiah (640–609). His contemporaries would have been Jeremiah, Zephaniah, and Habakkuk.

His name means "comfort" or "compassion," and his message of Assyria's doom would certainly have comforted the people of Judah who had suffered because of Assyria. The Assyrians had taken the northern kingdom of Israel in 722 and dispersed the people; and then they tried to take Judah in the days of Hezekiah (701), but were defeated by the angel of the Lord (Isa. 37). Assyria was always looming over the tiny kingdom of Judah, and having these ruthless people out of the way would have greatly bettered Judah's situation.

A Suggested Outline of the Book of Nahum

Theme: The vengeance of God on His enemies
Key verses: Nahum 1:2, 7

I. God Is Jealous: Nineveh Will Fall (Nahum 1:1–15)

    1. God declares His anger (Nahum 1:1–8)

    2. God speaks to Nineveh (Nahum 1:9–11, 14)

    3. God encourages Judah (Nahum 1:12–13, 15)

II. God Is Judge: How Nineveh Will Fall (Nahum 2:1–13)

    1. The invaders appear and advance (Nahum 2:1–4)

    2. The city is captured (Nahum 2:5–10)

    3. The conquerors taunt their captives (Nahum 2:11–13)

III. God Is Just: Why Nineveh Will Fall (Nahum 3:1–19)

    1. Her ruthless bloodshed (Nahum 3:1–3)

    2. Her idolatry (Nahum 3:4–7)

    3. Her pride and self-confidence (Nahum 3:8–19)

Chapter Eight

THE CITY IS NO MORE

(Nahum 1—3)

Queen Victoria was celebrating sixty years on the British throne when Rudyard Kipling published his poem "Recessional." Not everybody in Great Britain liked the poem because it punctured national pride at a time when the empire was at its peak. "Recessional" was a warning that other empires had vanished from the stage of history and England's might follow in their train. God was still the Judge of the nations. Kipling wrote,

> Far-called, our navies melt away;
> On dune and headland sinks the fire:
> Lo, all our pomp of yesterday
> Is one with Nineveh and Tyre!
> Judge of the Nations, spare us yet,
> Lest we forget—lest we forget!

The prophet Nahum would have applauded the poem, especially Kipling's reference to Nineveh, for it was Nahum who wrote the Old Testament book that vividly describes the destruction of Nineveh, the event that marked the beginning of the end for the Assyrian Empire.[1] Nahum made it clear that God is indeed the Judge of the nations, and that "pride goes before destruction, and a haughty spirit before a fall" (Prov. 16:18 NKJV). In the seventh century BC, the very mention of Nineveh brought fear to people's hearts, but today, Nineveh is mentioned primarily by Bible students, archeologists, and people interested in ancient history. *Sic transit gloria!*

In his brief book, Nahum makes three declarations about God and Nineveh.

1. GOD IS JEALOUS: NINEVEH WILL FALL (1:1–15)

The prophet characterizes his inspired message as both a "burden" and a "vision," something he felt and something he saw. The word translated "burden" simply means "to lift up" and was often used to describe prophetic messages that announced judgment. Isaiah used the word ten times in his prophecy as he wrote about "the burden of Babylon" (Isa. 13:1), "the burden of Moab" (15:1), etc. These burdens came as a result of the visions God gave His prophets ("seers") of dreadful events determined for the nations. It wasn't easy to be a prophet and see what lay in the future, and they felt the burden of their messages. Nineveh isn't mentioned by name until Nahum 2:8, but its destruction is the theme of the book.

God speaks of Himself (vv. 2–8). Three important words in this paragraph need to be understood because they all relate to the character of God: *jealousy, vengeance,* and *anger.*

Jealousy is a sin if it means being envious of what others have and wanting to possess it, but it's a virtue if it means cherishing what we have and wanting to protect it. A faithful husband and wife are jealous over one another and do everything they can to keep their relationship exclusive. "Jealous" and "zealous" come from the same root, for when you're jealous over someone, you're zealous to protect the relationship.

Since God made everything and owns everything, He is envious of no one, but since He is the only true God, He is jealous over His glory,

His name, and the worship and honor that are due to Him alone. In the second commandment, God prohibited the worship of idols and backed up the prohibition with this reason: "for I the Lord thy God am a jealous God" (Ex. 20:5).

When we studied the book of Hosea, we learned that the Lord was "married" to Israel in a covenant relationship, and any breach of that covenant aroused His jealous love. He will not share His people with false gods any more than a husband would share his wife with his neighbor. "For you shall worship no other god, for the Lord, whose name is Jealous, is a jealous God" (34:14 NKJV). "For the Lord your God is a consuming fire, a jealous God" (Deut. 4:24 NKJV; and see 6:15; 32:16, 21; 1 Kings 14:22). Nineveh was a city given over to iniquity, especially idolatry and cruelty, and God's jealous love burned against their pride and willful breaking of His law.

In Scripture, vengeance is usually presented as a sin. Both Jesus and Paul warned about it (Matt. 5:38–48; Rom. 12:17–21). But a just and holy God cannot see people flouting His law and do nothing about it. "It is mine to avenge; I will repay. … I will take vengeance on my adversaries and repay those who hate me" (Deut. 32:35, 41 NIV). God's people prayed to God to avenge them when other nations attacked them. "O Lord God, to whom vengeance belongs—O God, to whom vengeance belongs, shine forth!" (Ps. 94:1 NKJV). When God takes vengeance by judging people, it's because He is a holy God and is jealous (zealous) for His holy law.

God's anger isn't like human anger, which can be selfish and out of control. His is a holy anger, a righteous indignation against all that defies His authority and disobeys His law. God's people ought to exercise a holy anger against sin (Eph. 4:26), for, as Henry Ward Beecher said, "A person that does not know how to be angry does not know how to be good." He was speaking, of course, about righteous anger that opposes evil. If we can stand by and do nothing while innocent, helpless people are mistreated and exploited, then something is wrong with us. "Anger is one of the sinews of the soul," wrote Thomas Fuller. "He who lacks it has a maimed mind."

In Nahum 1:2, Nahum wrote that God was "furious" ("filled with wrath" NIV); and in verse 6, he described God's "indignation" as so fierce and powerful that it is "poured out like fire" with the power to "shatter" the rocks (NIV). However, verse 3 assures us that God's wrath isn't a fit of rage or a temper tantrum; for "the Lord is slow to anger" (see Jonah 4:2; Ex. 34:6; Num. 14:18).

God is so powerful that if His anger were not a holy anger, and if He were not "slow to anger," He could easily destroy everything. He controls the forces of nature (Nah. 1:3); He opened the Red Sea for the people of Israel to march through, and He can turn off the rain and make the most fruitful areas of the land languish (v. 4).[2] At Sinai, He made the mountain shake (Ex. 19:18), and when He pleases, He can cause the people of the world to tremble (Heb. 12:18–21).

The God that Nahum introduces to us is a jealous God who is angry at sin (Nah. 1:2), but He is also a good God who cares for His people (v. 7). Nahum invites us (as Paul put it) to "consider the goodness and severity of God" (Rom. 11:22 NKJV). "God is love" (1 John 4:8, 16), but He is also light (1:5), and His love is a holy love. He is a refuge for those who trust Him, but He is an "overwhelming flood" to those who are His enemies.

God speaks to Nineveh (vv. 9–11, 14). He informs the leaders of Assyria that He knows their plots (vv. 9, 11) and will cause all of their plans to fail. When the proud nations plot against God, He laughs at them and turns their schemes into confusion (Ps. 2:1–4). The Assyrians had plotted against Judah in the days of King Hezekiah, and God thwarted their plans (Isa. 36—37), but the Lord wouldn't allow this to happen a second time. Instead of marching out triumphantly, the leaders would be like drunks entangled in thorn bushes, and stubble burned in a prairie fire (Nah. 1:10).

The plotter mentioned in verse 11 is the king of Assyria, and God addresses him in verse 14, making three declarations: (1) his dynasty will end, because he will have no descendants; (2) the help of his gods and goddesses will end, because they will be destroyed; and (3) his life will end, because God will prepare his grave. What a solemn message for a man who was sure his plans would succeed! Why would God do all these things? The answer is plain: "You are vile!"

God speaks to Judah (vv. 12–13, 15). Although the Assyrian army outnumbered the army of Judah, and Assyria had more allies to help them fight, that didn't mean Assyria was bound to win, for God was fighting on behalf of Judah. Yes, the Lord had used Assyria to chasten Judah in the past, but that would not happen again.[3] This time, God would break the yoke and remove the shackles that Assyria had put on Judah, and Assyria would attack them no more.

In ancient days, news was carried by couriers, and the watchmen on the walls scanned the horizon hoping that messengers would bring good news. In this case, it was good news indeed: The courier would announce that Nineveh was fallen and the Assyrian army defeated and in disarray (v. 15).[4] Judah could now live in peace and enjoy her annual feasts and regular religious festivals.

You find this same statement in Isaiah 52:7, where the messenger announced the defeat of Babylon, and Paul quoted the verse in Romans 10:15 and applied it to the proclamation of the gospel to lost sinners. We don't usually think of feet as being beautiful, but they certainly are beautiful when they enable a messenger to carry good news that God has defeated our enemies. To Judah, it meant that Assyria was completely destroyed and could never again invade her land. To us who trust Christ, it means that He has completely defeated sin, death, and Satan, and that we are now free to enjoy the blessings of salvation.

2. GOD IS JUDGE: HOW NINEVEH WILL FALL (2:1–13)

In 612 BC, the Medes and the Babylonians united to attack Nineveh, and the Lord used them to judge the evil city. This chapter is a vivid description of what happened as seen by Nahum in the vision God gave him.

The invaders appear (vv. 1–4). The guards on the walls of the city see the army advancing and the officers issue orders and encourage their soldiers. You can almost hear the sharp commands: "Guard the fortress, watch the road, brace yourself, marshal all your strength!" (v. 1 NIV). Above all the noise, the voice of the Lord is heard as He speaks to Israel and Judah and assures them that they will be restored and reunited. (v. 2).[5]

The invading army is formidable with its man power, armor, weapons, and chariots (vv. 3–4). Already their shields are red with blood. The chariots look like flames of fire as they dash here and there in the streets of the city, and the soldiers find it easy to slaughter the defenseless people.

The city is captured (vv. 5–10). "He" in verse 5 refers to the king of Assyria, who had plotted against the Lord and His people (1:9). He gathers his best officers and gives them orders to protect the wall, but they are too late. They stumble like drunks instead of marching like heroes. The leaders were sure their fortress was impregnable, but their defenses proved to be their undoing.

The Khoser River flowed through the city, so the invaders dammed it up and then released the water so that it destroyed part of the wall and some of the buildings. It was a simple matter for the Medes and Babylonians to enter the city and take control. But they can't take credit for the victory; it was decreed by God that the city be destroyed, and the inhabitants be killed or taken captive (2:7). The invaders were but God's instruments to execute His will.

First, the soldiers line up the prisoners to march them off to their own lands, where they'll become slaves. Nahum compares the exodus to water draining out of a pool. Then the soldiers begin looting this fabulously wealthy city, and the people watch with dismay. "Hearts melt, knees give way, bodies tremble, every face grows pale" (v. 10 NIV). Nineveh is being treated the way she treated others; her sins had found her out.

The captive leaders are taunted (vv. 11–13). Speaking on behalf of God, the prophet has the last word. As the Assyrian captives are marched away, leaders and common citizens, and the city's treasures carried off by their captors, Nahum taunts the Ninevites by contrasting their present plight with their former glory.

The image of the lion was often used by the Assyrians in their art and architecture. Visit the Assyrian room in any large museum and you will see huge statues of lions. But even more, the Assyrians acted like lions as they stalked their prey and completely devoured their captives. "Where is the lions' den now?" Nahum asks as the city is destroyed. "Where is all your prey, the treasures you ruthlessly took from others?" Lions will normally take to their lair enough food for themselves and their cubs, but the Assyrians amassed wealth beyond measure, far more than they needed, and they did it at the cost of human lives.

No wonder the Lord announced, "I am against you" (v. 13 NIV). Over a century before, the Lord had sent Jonah to warn Nineveh, and when the city repented, He withdrew His hand of judgment. But now their time was up and the end had come. Assyria would be left with no weapons, no leaders, and no victories to be announced by their messengers. Instead, Assyria's enemies would hear the voice of couriers announcing peace because Assyria had been defeated (1:15).

3. GOD IS JUST: WHY NINEVEH WILL FALL (3:1–19)

"Shall not the Judge of all the earth do right?" (Gen. 18:25). God is long-suffering, but there comes a time when His hand of judgment falls. "You have rebuked the nations, You have destroyed the wicked; you have blotted out their name forever and ever" (Ps. 9:5 NKJV). Nahum gives three reasons why Nineveh deserved to be judged.

(1) Their ruthless bloodshed (vv. 1–3). The Assyrians were clever diplomats who lied to other nations and then broke their promises and destroyed them. They slaughtered people without regard for age or sex, and they stacked up corpses like lumber as warning to anybody who would oppose them. The shedding of innocent blood is a serious sin that God notes, remembers, and judges (Deut. 19:11–13; 2 Kings 21:16; 24:4; Ps. 106:38; Prov. 6:16–17; Isa. 59:7). Depraved dictators who authorize the heartless slaying of innocent victims will someday answer to God for their crimes against Him and humanity.

(2) Their idolatry (vv. 4–7). Often in Scripture, idolatry is associated with prostitution, and when you consider that the chief deity of Nineveh was Ishtar, goddess of sexual passion, fertility, and war, you can understand why Nahum used this metaphor. Because of their spiritual blindness, the Assyrians were ensnared by this evil goddess and were under the control of lust, greed, and violence. People become like the god that they worship (Ps. 115:8), for what we believe determines how we behave. Assyria spread this evil influence to other nations and enslaved them by their sorcery. (See the description of the corrupt end-times religious system given in Rev. 17.)

In ancient times, prostitutes were often shamed by being publicly exposed, and this is what God promised to do to Nineveh. God would expose Assyria's nakedness before all the nations, and this would be the end of their evil influence. The magnificent wealthy city would become a heap of ruins.

(3) Their pride and self-confidence (vv. 8–19). In this closing paragraph, Nahum uses a number of images to show the Assyrians their weaknesses and assure them of their ultimate defeat.

He begins with a fact of history: the defeat of the Egyptian city of Thebes, or No-Ammon, by the Assyrians, in 663 (vv. 8–11). If you visit Karnak and Luxor in Upper Egypt, you will be at the site of ancient Thebes. This capital city of Upper Egypt was sure it was safe from any invader, yet it went down in defeat before Assyria. Like Nineveh, Thebes was situated by waters that were supposed to be their defense, but the city fell just the same. Thebes had many allies, but they couldn't protect her.

What Assyria did to the people of Thebes would in turn be done to them: Their children would be dashed to pieces, the leaders would become slaves, and the people would become exiles. Now, argues Nahum, if this happened to Thebes, why couldn't it happen to Nineveh? Their pride and self-confidence would be totally destroyed as the Medes and Babylonians captured the city. Nineveh would drink the cup of God's wrath and become drunk (v. 11; see Ps. 75:8; Isa. 51:17; Jer. 25:14ff.).

In fact, the conquest would be so easy, it would be like ripe figs dropping into a person's mouth (Nah. 3:12). Why? Because the ferocious Assyrian soldiers would be drained of their strength and be like women: weak, afraid, and unable to meet the enemy (vv. 13–14).[6] They wouldn't be able to bar the gates or stop the enemy from setting fire to them, nor would they be able to repair the walls or carry water to put out the fires.

The next image is that of insects (vv. 15–17). The invading soldiers would sweep through the land and the city like a plague of grasshoppers or locusts and wipe everything out. The Babylonian merchants were also like locusts as they collected all the treasures they could find. But the Assyrian leaders were like locusts that go to sleep on the wall on a cold day, but when the sun comes up, they feel the heat and fly away. The king and his council were overconfident, like locusts sleeping on the wall, but when the invasion occurred, they flew off to a safe place!

Assyria was like a scattered flock with sleeping shepherds (v. 18), or like a wounded body with no way to be healed (v. 19a). They had no allies to rescue them, for all the other nations would rejoice when they heard that the Assyrian Empire was no more (v. 19b).

Like the book of Jonah, the book of Nahum ends with a question: "for who has not felt your endless cruelty?" (v. 19 NIV). Nahum emphasizes the same truth that was declared by the prophet Amos: God punishes cruel nations that follow inhumane policies and brutal practices (Amos 1—2). Whether it's practicing genocide, exploiting the poor, supporting slavery, or failing to provide people with the necessities of life, the sins of national leaders are known by God, and He eventually judges.

If you question that fact, go and search for Nineveh.

QUESTIONS FOR PERSONAL REFLECTION
OR GROUP DISCUSSION

1. Give an example of good jealousy, and an example of bad jealousy.

2. How do you feel when you read that God is jealous? Why?

3. How can God be jealous but not envious? What is the difference?

4. What are some danger signs of human anger?

5. How can God's anger always be right when ours is so often wrong?

6. How can our anger be transformed to be more like God's? What is our part in the process?

7. How do you understand God's pity and compassion alongside His jealousy, anger, and wrath?

8. As you observe your neighbors or relatives, would you say they deserve God's judgment? Why or why not? How does God see them?

9. According to Wiersbe, what are the three reasons Nahum gives why Nineveh deserves to be judged (Nahum 3)?

10. Wiersbe states that "people become like the god that they worship (Ps. 115:8), for what we believe determines how we behave." If you look at the behavior of non-Christians around you, what would you say they worship? What about the behavior of people who attend your church?

HABAKKUK IN HIS TIME

Habakkuk was a contemporary of Nahum, Zephaniah, and Jeremiah, which places him in the reigns of Josiah (640–609 BC) and Jehoiakim (609–598). Assyria was off the scene, but Babylon ("the Chaldeans") was in power. Nebuchadnezzar had defeated Egypt in 605 and was about to attack Judah. Jeremiah had announced that Babylon would invade Judah, destroy Jerusalem and the temple, and send the nation into exile; and this happened in 606–586.

Habakkuk's little book indicates that he knew the Old Testament Scriptures well, was a competent theologian, and had a great faith in God. Because of the psalm in chapter 3, some scholars think he may have been a priest who led worship in the temple. If so, then like Jeremiah and Ezekiel, he was a priest called to be a prophet, which is a much more difficult ministry.

His name means "to embrace" or "to wrestle," and in his book, he does both. He wrestles with God concerning the problem of how a holy God could use a wicked nation like Babylon to chasten the people of Judah; and then by faith, he embraces God and clings to His promises. Habakkuk also wrestles with the spiritual decline of the nation and why God wasn't doing something about it. Habakkuk wanted to see the people revived (3:2), but God wasn't answering his prayers.

The prophet's statement "The just shall live by his faith" (2:4) is quoted three times in the New Testament (Rom. 1:17; Gal. 3:11; Heb. 10:38). The emphasis in Romans is on *the just*, in Galatians on how they should *live*, and in Hebrews on *"by faith."* It takes three books to explain and apply this one verse!

A SUGGESTED OUTLINE OF THE BOOK OF HABAKKUK

Theme: The just shall live by faith.
Key verse: Habakkuk 2:4

I. The Prophet Wondering and Worrying (Habakkuk 1)
    1. God is indifferent (Habakkuk 1:2–4)
       God's reply: I am working (Habakkuk 1:5–11)
    2. God is inconsistent (Habakkuk 1:12–17)

II. The Prophet Watching and Waiting (Habakkuk 2)
    1. Write God's vision (Habakkuk 2:1–3)
    2. Trust God's Word (Habakkuk 2:4–5)
       The just shall live by faith (Habakkuk 2:4)[1]
    3. Declare God's judgment (Habakkuk 2:6–20)
       (1) Woe to the selfish (Habakkuk 2:6–8)
       (2) Woe to the covetous (Habakkuk 2:9–11)
       (3) Woe to the exploiters (Habakkuk 2:12–14)
          God's glory will fill the earth (Habakkuk 2:14)
       (4) Woe to the drunkards (Habakkuk 2:15–17)
       (5) Woe to the idolaters (Habakkuk 2:18–20)
       God is still on His throne (Habakkuk 2:20)

III. The Prophet Worshipping and Witnessing (Habakkuk 3)
    1. He prays to God (Habakkuk 3:1–2)
    2. He ponders God's ways (Habakkuk 3:3–15)
    3. He praises God (Habakkuk 3:16–19)

Chapter Nine

THE PROPHET WORRYING

(Habakkuk 1)

One of the modern "Christian myths" that ought to be silenced says that when you trust Jesus Christ, you get rid of all your problems. You don't.

It's true that your basic spiritual problem—your relationship with God—has been solved, but with that solution comes a whole new set of problems that you didn't face when you were an unbeliever, like "Why do good people suffer and evil people prosper?" or "Why isn't God answering my prayer?" or "When I'm doing my best for the Lord, why do I experience the worst from others?"

Christians who claim to be without problems are either not telling the truth or not growing and experiencing real life. Perhaps they're just not thinking at all. They're living in a religious dream world that has blocked out reality and stifled honest feelings. Like Job's uncomfortable comforters, they mistake shallow optimism for the peace of God and "the good life" for the blessing of God. You never hear them ask what David and Jesus asked, "My God, my God, why hast thou forsaken me?" (Ps. 22:1; Matt. 27:46).

Habakkuk wasn't that kind of a believer. As he surveyed the land of Judah and then watched the international scene, he found himself struggling with some serious problems. But he did the right thing: He took his problems to the Lord.

"WHY IS GOD SO INDIFFERENT?" (1:2–11)

Being a perceptive man, Habakkuk knew the kingdom of Judah was rapidly deteriorating. Ever since the death of King Josiah in 609 BC, his religious reforms had been forgotten and his son and successor Jehoiakim had been leading the nation closer to disaster. (If you want to know what God thought about Jehoiakim, read Jer. 22:13–19.)

The prophet's concern (vv. 2–3). Habakkuk's vocabulary in this chapter indicates that times were difficult and dangerous, for he uses words like *violence, iniquity, grievance* (misery), *spoiling* (destruction), *strife, contention* (disputes), and *injustice*. Habakkuk prayed that God would do something about the violence, strife, and injustice in the land, but God didn't seem to hear. In verse 2, the first word translated "cry" simply means "to call for help," but the second word means "to scream, to cry with a loud voice, to cry with a disturbed heart." As he prayed about the wickedness in the land, Habakkuk became more and more burdened and wondered why God seemed so indifferent.

The basic cause (v. 4). The nation's problems were caused by leaders who wouldn't obey the law. "Therefore the law is paralyzed, and justice never prevails. The wicked hem in the righteous, so that justice is perverted" (v. 4 NIV). The rich exploited the poor and escaped punishment by bribing the officials. The law was either ignored or twisted, and nobody seemed to care. The courts were crooked, officials were interested only in money, and the admonition in Exodus 23:6–8 was completely unheeded.

The Lord's counsel (vv. 5–11). God answered His servant and assured him that He was at work among the nations even though Habakkuk couldn't see it.[1] God gave Habakkuk a revelation, not an explanation, for what we always need in times of doubt is a new view of God. The Lord doesn't owe us any explanations, but He does graciously reveal Himself and His work to those who seek Him.[2]

What God was doing was so amazing, incredible, and unheard of that even His prophet would be shocked: God was planning to punish the Jews by using the godless Babylonians! They were a "ruthless and impetuous people" (v. 6 NIV), "a feared and dreaded people" who were a law unto themselves and afraid of nobody (v. 7 NIV). Their only purpose was to promote themselves and conquer and enslave other peoples.

The Lord then used a number of pictures from nature to describe the Babylonians and how they treated people. Their horses had the speed of leopards and the ferocity of wolves, and their troops swooped down on their prey like vultures. Their army swept across the desert like the wind and gathered and deported prisoners the way a man digs sand and ships it to a foreign land.

Could anything stop them? Certainly God could stop them, but He was the One who was enlisting their aid! Nothing human could hinder their progress. The Babylonians had no respect for authority, whether kings or generals. (One of their practices was to put captured kings in cages and exhibit them like animals.) They laughed at gates and walls as they built their siege ramps and captured fortified cities. They worshipped the god of power and depended wholly on their own strength.

Habakkuk learned that God was not indifferent to the sins of the people of Judah. The Lord was planning to chasten Judah by allowing the Babylonians to invade the land and take them into exile.[3] This wasn't the answer Habakkuk was expecting. He was hoping God would send a revival to His people (see 3:2), judge the evil leaders, and establish righteousness in the land. Then the nation would escape punishment and the people and cities would be spared.

However, God had warned His people time and time again, but they wouldn't listen. Prophet after prophet had declared the Word (2 Chron. 36:14–21), only to be rejected, and He had sent natural calamities like droughts and plagues, and various military defeats, but the people wouldn't listen. Instead of repenting, the people hardened their hearts even more and turned for help to the gods of the nations around them. They had tried God's long-suffering long enough, and it was time for God to act.

"How Could God Be So Inconsistent?" (1:12–17)

As far as Habakkuk was concerned, God's first answer hadn't been an answer at all. In fact, it only created a new problem that was even more puzzling: inconsistency on the part of God. How could a holy God use a wicked nation to punish His own special people?

The holiness of God (vv. 12–13). The prophet focused on the character of God, as Jonah had done when he disagreed with what God was doing (Jonah 4:2). "Men of faith are always the men who have to confront problems," wrote G. Campbell Morgan, for if you believe in God, you sometimes wonder why He allows certain things to happen. But keep in mind that there's a difference between doubt and unbelief. Like Habakkuk, the doubter questions God and may even debate with God, but the doubter doesn't abandon God. But unbelief is rebellion against God, a refusal to accept what He says and does. Unbelief is an act of the will, while doubt is born out of a troubled mind and a broken heart.

Habakkuk's argument with God is a short course in theology. He started with the fact of the holiness of God. The Babylonians were far more wicked sinners than the people in Judah, so how could God use evil, idolatrous Gentiles to punish His own chosen people? Yes, His people deserved punishment, but couldn't God find a better instrument? Would this mean the end of the nation? No, for "we shall not die" (Hab. 1:12). God had purposes to fulfill through the Jewish nation, and He would preserve His people, but they would experience painful trials.

The prophet needed to remember two facts: (1) God had used other tools to chasten His people—war, natural calamities, the preaching of the prophets—and the people wouldn't listen; (2) the greater the light, the greater the responsibility. Yes, the Babylonians were wicked sinners, but they were idolaters who didn't know the true and living God. This didn't excuse their sins (Rom. 1:18ff.), but it did explain their conduct. The Jews claimed to know the Lord, and yet they were sinning against the very law they claimed to believe! Sin in the life of a believer is far worse than sin in the life of an unbeliever. When God's people deliberately disobey Him, they sin against a flood of light and an ocean of love.

Habakkuk reminded God that He was eternal, and therefore knew the end from the beginning and couldn't be caught by surprise. He was the Mighty God ("Rock" NIV) who had all power and never changed. So, what about His covenants with the Jews? What about His special promises? As a holy God, He couldn't look with approval on sin (Hab. 1:13); yet He was "tolerant" of sin in the land of Judah and "silent" as the Babylonians prepared to swallow up His people! Habakkuk wanted God to say something and do something, but God was silent and seemingly inactive.

Keep in mind that this wasn't simply a national problem to Habakkuk, or a theological problem; it was a personal problem as he cried out, "My God, my Holy One" (v. 12 NIV). National and international events were affecting his personal walk with God, and this concerned him greatly. But wrestling with these challenges is the only way for our "faith muscles" to grow. To avoid tough questions, or to settle for half-truths and superficial pat answers it to remain immature, but to face questions honestly and talk them through with the Lord is to grow in grace and in the knowledge of Christ (2 Peter 3:18).[4]

The helplessness of the people (vv. 14–15). After presenting his case on the basis of the holiness of God, Habakkuk argued from the viewpoint of the helplessness of the people (vv. 14–15). Judah could never survive an attack from the savage Babylonians. To the Babylonians, life was cheap, and prisoners of war were expendable. People were like fish to be hooked or sea creatures to be trapped.

How could God allow His weak people to be invaded by such a heartless and ruthless nation? Of course, the false prophets in Judah were saying, "It can't happen here" (see Jer. 6:14; 8:11; 14:13ff.), but their blind optimism would soon be exposed as lies. For forty years, the prophet Jeremiah warned the people of Judah and begged them to turn back to God, but they refused to listen. What Judah needed wasn't great military strength but obedient faith in God.

The haughtiness of the enemy (vv. 16–17). The prophet's third approach was to point out the way the Babylonians lived and worshipped. They trusted in their mighty military machine ("their net," vv. 16–17) and worshipped the gods of power (see v. 11) and violence. The Babylonians were "puffed up" (2:4 NIV) with arrogance and self-confidence. How could God honor them by giving them a victory over Judah? God was filling their net with victims, and the Chaldeans were emptying the net by destroying one nation after another (1:17 NIV).

Habakkuk could have said more about the abominable religion of the Babylonians. They believed in a multitude of gods and goddesses, with Bel as the head of their pantheon. Anu was the god of the sky, Nebo the god of literature and wisdom, and Nergal was the sun god. Sorcery was an important part of their religion, including honoring Ea, the god of magic. Their priests practiced divination and consulted omens, all of which was prohibited by the law of Moses. It seemed unreasonable that the Lord would allow such spiritually ignorant people to conquer Judah, the land that housed His own temple.

Habakkuk finished his defense and waited for God to speak. Like a servant, he stood waiting and watching (2:1), wondering how God would respond to his "complaint" (NIV). The answer God gave is recorded in chapter 2.

But before we listen to God's encouraging reply, we must pause to examine our own hearts. Are we fully yielded to God and willing for Him to have His way with us and with those whom we love? There's nothing wrong with wrestling with the problems of life and seeking a better understanding of God's will, but we must beware lest we start debating with God and trying to change His mind.

We admire Habakkuk for being an honest man and wanting God to spare the people he loved. We want to imitate him in his openness and sincerity and in his willingness to wait for God's answer. But we want to remember what Paul wrote to the believers in Rome:

> Oh, the depth of the riches both of the wisdom
> and knowledge of God! How unsearchable are His
> judgments and His ways past finding out! For who has
> known the mind of the Lord? Or who has become His
> counselor? Or who has first given to Him and it shall
> be repaid to him? For of Him and through Him and to
> Him are all things, to whom be glory forever. Amen.

ROMANS 11:33–36 NKJV

QUESTIONS FOR PERSONAL REFLECTION
OR GROUP DISCUSSION

1. When you look around your country today, what feelings or questions do you have?

2. What problems were solved when you became a believer? What new problems have you faced since you became a believer?

3. What do you usually do when you are struggling with problems? What do you think you should do?

4. Habakkuk's cry (1:2) meant "to call for help" but then became "to scream, to cry with a loud voice, to cry with a disturbed heart." When have you experienced something like this?

5. God gave Habakkuk a revelation instead of an explanation. What is the difference?

6. What answer did Habakkuk expect to hear as he waited on the Lord (1:5–11)? When have you cried to the Lord and He answered in a way you were not expecting?

7. Habakkuk debated with God without abandoning Him. Have you debated with God? If so, did you feel like you were abandoning Him when you brought up the issue in question?

8. Have you ever wondered how a good and holy God could allow something? If so, when? What were the circumstances?

9. Wiersbe writes, "The greater the light, the greater the responsibility." How was this true in Israel's case? How is it true for us?

10. In Habakkuk 1:13, we see a timeless question. What answer would you give to someone who was wrestling with this?

Chapter Ten

THE PROPHET WATCHING AND WAITING

(Habakkuk 2)

This chapter reports an experience Habakkuk had that is similar to one recorded by Asaph the psalmist in Psalm 73. Like Habakkuk, Asaph was bewildered at the providential working of God in this world: He was disturbed because the wicked seemed to be prospering, while the righteous were suffering. Like Habakkuk, he reasoned with God, and then, like Habakkuk, he gave God the opportunity to reply.

"When I thought to know this," he wrote, "it was too painful for me; until I went into the sanctuary of God" (Ps. 73:16–17). There in the sanctuary he found God's answer to his problem, and his sighing was turning into singing.

Let's join Habakkuk on the watchtower, which was his sanctuary, and listen to what the Lord said to him. When God did speak to His servant, He gave him three responsibilities to fulfill.

1. WRITE GOD'S VISION (2:1–3)

The prophet saw himself as a watchman on the walls of Jerusalem, waiting for a message from God that he could share with the people. In ancient days, the watchmen were responsible to warn the city of approaching danger, and if they weren't faithful, their hands would be stained with the blood of the people who died (Ezek. 3:17–21; 33:1–3). It was a serious responsibility.

The image of the watchman carries a spiritual lesson for us today. As God's people, we know that danger is approaching, and it's our responsibility to warn people to "flee from the wrath to come" (Matt. 3:7). If we don't share the gospel with lost sinners, then their blood may be on our hands. We want to be able to say with Paul, "Therefore I testify to you this day that I am innocent of the blood of all men" (Acts 20:26 NKJV).

You get the impression that Habakkuk was fearful of what the Lord might say to him because of His servant's "complaint" (Hab. 2:1 NIV). But the Lord graciously answered Habakkuk and gave him the vision he needed to turn his worrying into worshipping. This vision included not only the words in Habakkuk 2, but also the revelation of God's glory recorded in 3:3–15. When you behold the glory of God and believe the Word of God, it gives you faith to accept the will of God.

We wouldn't be studying this book today had Habakkuk not obeyed God's orders and written down what God had told him and shown him. This writing was to be permanent so that generation after generation could read it. It was also to be plain, written so that anybody could read it, and it was to be public so that even somebody running past the tablets on display could get the message immediately.[1] Habakkuk wasn't the only person in Judah who needed this message, and it was his obligation to share it.

The revelation God gave was for a future time and about a future time. While the immediate application was to the end of the Babylonian captivity, the writer of the epistle to the Hebrews interpreted it to refer also to the return of Jesus Christ. Led by the Holy Spirit, he changed "it" to "he" and applied it to our Lord (Hab. 2:3). "For yet a little while, and he that shall come will come, and will not tarry" (Heb. 10:37). Along with the scoffers Peter wrote about, some readers might ask, "Where is the promise of his coming?" (2 Peter 3:3ff.), and God's reply is, "Wait for it! It will surely come!" A discouraged Jew in Babylonian exile might ask, "Will the Lord come and deliver us?" and the answer is, "Yes! Wait for Him!"

2. TRUST GOD'S WORD (2:4–5)

The contrast here is between people of faith and people who arrogantly trust themselves and leave God out of their lives. The immediate application was to the Babylonians.

The sinner. The Babylonians were "puffed up" with pride over their military might and their great achievements. They had built an impressive empire, which they were sure was invincible. The words of Nebuchadnezzar express it perfectly: "Is not this great Babylon, that I have built for a royal dwelling by my mighty power and for the honor of my majesty?" (Dan. 4:30 NKJV).

But Nebuchadnezzar and the Babylonians aren't the only ones puffed up with pride and self-sufficiency. This is the condition of most of the people in today's society who belong to the world and live for the world. The apostle John warns us against "the pride [vain glory] of life" that belongs to this present evil world system, which is against God and without God (1 John 2:15–17).

Besides puffing them up, what else does pride do to people? It twists them inwardly, for the soul of the unbeliever is "not upright," which means his inner appetites are crooked and sinful. He delights in the things that God abhors, the things God condemns in the five "woes" in this chapter. One of the chief causes of the corruption in this world is what Peter calls "lust" (2 Peter 1:4), which simply means "evil desires, passionate longing." Were it not for the base appetites of people, longing to be satisfied but never satisfied, the "sin industries" would never prosper.

Pride also makes people restless: They're never satisfied (Hab. 2:5). That's why they're given over to whine, never at rest, never satisfied.

They're constantly seeking for some new experience to thrill them or some new achievement to make them important. Pride makes us greedy. The Babylonians weren't satisfied with what they had; they coveted even more land and wealth, and therefore set their course to conquer every nation that stood in their way. More than one king or dictator in history has followed this resolve, only to discover that it leads to disappointment, ruin, and death.

The just. Now for the contrast: "The just shall live by his faith" (v. 4b; see Rom. 1:17; Gal. 3:11; Heb. 10:38). This is the first of three wonderful assurances that God gives in this chapter to encourage His people. This one emphasizes God's grace, because grace and faith always go together. Habakkuk 2:14 emphasizes God's glory and assures us that, though this world is now filled with violence and corruption (Gen. 6:5, 11–13), it shall one day be filled with God's glory. The third assurance is in Habakkuk 2:20 and emphasizes God's government. Empires may rise and fall, but God is on His holy throne, and He is King of Kings and Lord of Lords.

"The just shall live by his faith" was the watchword of the Reformation, and they may well be the seven most important monosyllables in all of church history. It was verse 4, quoted in Romans 1:17, that helped to lead Martin Luther into the truth of justification by faith. "This text," said Luther, "was to me the true gate of Paradise."

Justification is the gracious act of God whereby He declares the believing sinner righteous and gives that believing sinner a perfect standing in Jesus Christ. The "just" person isn't someone who has met all of God's requirements by means of good works, "For by the works of the law shall no flesh be justified" (Gal. 2:16; see Rom. 3:20). "For if righteousness comes through the law, then Christ died in vain" (Gal. 2:21 NKJV).

Our Lord's parable of the Pharisee and the publican makes it clear that no amount of religious effort can save a lost sinner (Luke 18:9–14). We can't justify ourselves before God because we stand with the whole world, guilty and condemned before His throne (Rom. 3:19). All we can do is put saving faith in Jesus Christ and His work on the cross, because that is the only way to be saved. "Therefore being justified by faith, we have peace with God through our Lord Jesus Christ" (Rom. 5:1).

The victory. We are not only saved by faith (Eph. 2:8–9), but we are instructed to live by faith. "And this is the victory that has overcome the world—our faith" (1 John 5:4 NKJV). Faith is a lifestyle that is just the opposite of being "puffed up" and depending on your own resources. Habakkuk knew that difficult times were coming to the people of Judah, and their only resource was to trust God's Word and rest in His will.

Living by faith is the major theme of the book of Hebrews (Heb. 10:38), for in that book the phrase "by faith" is found over twenty times. To live by faith means to believe God's Word and obey it no matter how we feel, what we see, or what the consequences may be. This is illustrated in Hebrews 11, the famous "by faith" chapter of the Bible. The men and women mentioned in that chapter were ordinary people, but they accomplished extraordinary things because they trusted God and did what He told them to do. It has well been said that faith is not believing in spite of evidence; it's obeying in spite of consequence, resting on God's faithfulness.

3. DECLARE GOD'S JUDGMENT (2:6–20)

To the faithful Jews in the land, God would be a refuge and strength (Nah. 1:7; Ps. 46), but to the godless Babylonians invading the land, He would be a judge and eventually punish their sins and give them what they deserved. In this "taunt song," God pronounces "woe" upon five different sins, all of which are prevalent in the world today.

(1) Selfish ambition (vv. 6–8). Of itself, ambition can be a good thing, but if it motivates people to be greedy, selfish, and abusive, it's a bad thing. "It has always been my ambition to preach the gospel where Christ was not known," wrote Paul (Rom. 15:20 NIV), and God honored that holy ambition. Paul also wrote, "Therefore we also have as our ambition ... to be pleasing to Him" (2 Cor. 5:9 NASB), an ambition we all should imitate.

The Babylonians were consumed by selfish ambition, and they stopped at nothing to acquire wealth and expand their kingdom. They had hoards of stolen goods, plundered from helpless people. God warned them that the owners of this wealth would one day rise up to condemn them and collect what was due.[2] Then the Babylonians will become the victims! This happened when the Medes and the Persians invaded Babylon and overthrew Belshazzar (Dan. 5). Babylon plundered other nations, and she herself was plundered. Babylon had shed rivers of blood, and her blood was shed. It's a basic law of the universe that eventually we reap what we sow.

(2) Covetousness (vv. 9–11). According to Ephesians 4:28, there are three ways to get wealth: You can work for it, steal it, or receive it as a gift. Stealing is wrong because the eighth commandment says, "Thou shalt not steal" (Ex. 20:15). The Babylonians took land that wasn't theirs in order to build an empire that glorified them and assured them safety. Their goal was security, like the eagle's nest on the high mountain crags. Of course, this was a false security, because no individual or nation can build walls high enough to keep God out.

What will be the consequences of this covetousness? Instead of having houses and families that bring honor, they will have disgrace and shame and will eventually lose their lives. "For what shall it profit a man, if he shall gain the whole world, and lose his own soul?" (Mark 8:36). The very materials in their expensive houses would testify against them, for they were plundered from helpless people. James used a similar image when he warned the rich that the wages they owed their laborers would witness against them at the judgment (James 5:1–6).[3]

It's likely that some of the covetous Jews felt the sting of this rebuke, for they were amassing fortunes by exploiting the poor and using that money to build expensive houses. (See Amos 3:15; 6:11.) The prophets often rebuked the rich because they lived in luxury, while the poor suffered. Jesus warned His disciples, "Take heed, and beware of covetousness" (Luke 12:15), and that warning is valid today. "Thou shalt not covet" may be the last of the Ten Commandments (Ex. 20:17), but if we're guilty of covetousness, we're in danger of breaking the other nine!

(3) Exploitation of people (vv. 12–14). Babylon was built by bloodshed, the blood of innocent victims. It was built by prisoners of war, slave labor that was exploited to the fullest extent. Babylon was proud of what she had built, but God said it wouldn't last; it was only fuel for the fire. The city of Babylon was an architectural marvel, but their great projects were for nothing. It's all gone, and today, if you want to see what Babylon was like, you have to visit a museum.

When I was a seminary student in Chicago, one of our classes did just that: We visited a museum to see the exhibit on Babylon. I recall how impressed I was with the model of the city, marveling that such magnificent walls and gates and buildings could be constructed in those ancient days. But my wonder turned to disgust when I recalled that the city was built with slave labor and that the soul of one of those slaves meant more to God than all the buildings put together.

In contrast to the shame and infamy of Babylon, God promised that His glory would one day cover the earth (v. 14). The "glory" of Babylon didn't last, but the glory of the Lord will abide forever. Certainly, the Lord was glorified when Babylon fell before her enemies in 539 BC (see Jer. 50—51), and He will be glorified when the Babylon of the last days is destroyed, that final great world empire that opposes God (Rev. 17—18). When Jesus Christ returns and establishes His kingdom, then God's glory will indeed cover the whole earth (Isa. 11:1–9).[4]

The fall of "Babylon the great" is a reminder to us that what man builds without God can never last. The exploiter will eventually lose everything, and man's "utopias" will turn out to be disasters. We can't exploit people made in God's image and expect to escape God's judgment. It may take time, but eventually the judgment falls.

(4) Drunkenness and violence (vv. 15–17). This repulsive picture can be interpreted both personally and nationally. While the Bible doesn't demand total abstinence, it does warn against the evils of strong drink (Prov. 20:1; 21:17; 23:20–21, 29–35; Rom. 13:13; Gal. 5:21; 1 Thess. 5:7). Drunkenness and sensual behavior often go together (Gen. 9:20–27; 19:30–38; Rom. 13:11–14).

But the word *neighbor* could also refer to a neighboring nation that was "intoxicated" by Babylon's power and made naked before Babylon's invading armies. In Scripture, drinking a cup of wine can be a picture of judgment (Jer. 25:15ff.), and nakedness sometimes speaks of the devastating effects of military invasion (Isa. 47:1–3).

However, what Babylon did to others, God would do to her. Babylon had been a golden cup in God's hands (Jer. 51:7), and He had used her to chasten the nations, but now God will give her a cup to drink that will bring her to ruin (see Rev. 16:19).[5] She will be ashamed as other nations look on her nakedness. Divine retribution will be hers: The violence she did to others will be done to her; as she shed the blood of others, her blood will be shed; and as she destroyed the lands of other nations, so her land will be devastated. The glory of God will cover the earth, but Babylon's "glory" will be covered with shame. The picture is that of a repulsive drunk vomiting all over himself, and it isn't a very pretty picture.

It's worth noting that God mentions the way the Babylonians abused trees and animals (Hab. 2:17), suggesting that the soldiers wastefully chopped down trees and killed cattle to use both the wood and the meat for their war effort. God also mentions His concern for animals in Jonah 4:11, so check the references. You wonder how many birds and animals lost either their lives or their homes because of this policy. (See Deut. 20:19–20 for Israel's policy on war supplies.)

(5) Idolatry (vv. 18–20). Sad to say, the people of Judah were also guilty of this sin, for during the declining years of the kingdom, they worshipped the gods of the other nations. All the prophets cried out against this flagrant violation of the second commandment (Ex. 20:4–6), but the people refused to repent.

What is idolatry? Romans 1:25 gives the best answer: worshipping and serving the creature instead of the Creator. It started with Lucifer who said, "I will be like the most High" (Isa. 14:14), and it entered humanity when Satan tempted Eve with, "You will be like God" (Gen. 3:5 NKJV). It's the popular philosophy of the world that man is the highest thing in the universe and can pull himself up by his own bootstraps to any level he chooses. "Glory to man in the highest!"

Not only is idolatry disobedience to God's Word, but it's also foolish and useless. Of what value is a god made by a man? It's much more reasonable to worship the God who made the man! (See Rom. 1:18ff.) Not only is the idol useless (see Ps. 115), but it does definite evil by teaching lies (Hab. 2:18) and giving people false confidence that the dumb idol can help them. For a heartbreaking example of this kind of foolish reasoning, read Jeremiah 44.

Idols are dead substitutes for the living God (Ps. 115). Whatever people delight in other than God, whatever they are devoted to and sacrifice for, whatever they couldn't bear to be without, is an idol and therefore under the condemnation of God. Most people in civilized countries don't worship man-made images of things in nature, but if the above definition is correct, modern society has its idols just as the Babylonians did.

Famous people are the "idols" of millions, especially politicians, athletes, wealthy tycoons, and actors and actresses. Even dead entertainers like Marilyn Monroe, James Dean, and Elvis Presley still have their followers. People may also worship and serve man-made things like cars, houses, boats, jewelry, and art. While all of us appreciate beautiful and useful things, it's one thing to own them and quite something else to be owned by them. Albert Schweitzer said, "Anything you have that you cannot give away, you do not really own; it owns you." I've met people who so idolized their children and grandchildren that they refused to let them consider giving their lives for Christian service.

Social position can be an idol and so can vocation achievement. For some people, their god is their appetite (Phil. 3:19; Rom. 16:18); and they live only to experience carnal pleasures. Intellectual ability can be a terrible idol (2 Cor. 10:5) as people worship their IQ and refuse to submit to God's Word.

God ended His reply to Habakkuk by giving a third assurance: "But the Lord is in his holy temple: let all the earth keep silence before him" (Hab. 2:20; see Ps. 11:4). The first assurance focused on God's grace (Hab. 2:4), and the second on God's glory (v. 14). This third assurance focuses on God's government; God is on the throne and has everything under control. Therefore, we shouldn't complain against God or question what He's doing. Like faithful servants, we must simply stand and listen for His commands. "Be still, and know that I am God" (Ps. 46:10).

Seeing the vision of God and hearing the voice of God made a tremendous difference in Habakkuk's life. As he grasped the significance of the three great assurances God gave him, he was transformed from being a worrier and a watcher to being a worshipper. In the closing chapter of this book, he will share with us the vision he had of God and the difference it made in his life.

QUESTIONS FOR PERSONAL REFLECTION
OR GROUP DISCUSSION

1. Have you ever foreseen something bad that was going to happen that other people were ignoring? If so, how did that feel? Or if you haven't, how do you think it would feel?

2. As you look at the non-Christians around you, do you foresee disaster for them because they don't know Christ? If so, what do you do about that? If not, explain.

3. What can hold us back from proclaiming a warning to those who are ignoring God?

4. Pride puffs people up about their achievements, twists their moral values, and makes them never satisfied with what they own and always restless for another thrill or achievement (2:4–5). Are you prone to any of these faults? If so, which ones?

5. What is justification? Who are "the just" (2:4)?

6. What does it mean to "live by faith" (see 2:4)?

7. Which five sins does God pronounce woe on in 2:6–20? Which of those do you see most often in the world around you?

8. How would you define *ambition*? What are its positive and negative characteristics?

9. What is covetousness? Where do you see it in your life? What attitude is the antidote to covetousness?

10. What is the definition of an idol? What are some examples today? What are the similarities and differences between a carved wooden idol in a temple and the idol of materialism?

11. What are the three assurances God gave to Habakkuk in the midst of the "woes" (see 2:4, 14, 20)? Which of these assurances means the most to you right now?

Chapter Eleven

THE PROPHET WORSHIPPING

(Habakkuk 3)

When Habakkuk started his book, he was "down in the valley," wrestling with the will of God. Then he climbed higher and stood on the watchtower, waiting for God to reply. After hearing God's Word and seeing God's glory, he became like a deer bounding confidently on the mountain heights (3:19)! His circumstances hadn't changed, but he had changed, and now he was walking by faith instead of sight. He was living by promises, not explanations.

It isn't easy to climb higher in the life of faith, but who wants to live in the valley? Like Habakkuk, we must honestly talk to God about our difficulties, we must pray, we must meditate on God's Word, and we must be willing to experience fear and trembling as the Lord reveals Himself to us (v. 16). But it will be worth it as we reach new summits of faith and discover new opportunities for growth and service.

What took Habakkuk from the valley to the summit? The same spiritual disciplines that can take us there: prayer, vision, and faith. Habakkuk interceded for God's work (vv. 1–2), pondered God's ways (vv. 3–15), and affirmed God's will (vv. 16–19).

PRAYER: PRAY FOR THE WORK OF GOD (3:1–2)

This chapter is a "prayer psalm" that may have been used in the temple worship in Jerusalem.[1] (For the other "prayer psalms," see Ps. 17; 86; 90; 102; and 142.) The prophet was now praying to the Lord and not arguing with the Lord, and his prayer soon became praise and worship.

He prayed because he had heard God speak. The word *speech* means "report" and refers to what God had told him earlier (Hab. 2:2–3). Knowing the will of God should motivate us to pray "Thy will be done." The same God who ordains the end also ordains the means to the end, and prayer is an important part of that means. "You do not have because you do not ask" (James 4:2 NKJV).

Also, hearing God's Word generates faith in the heart of the child of God (Rom. 10:17), and without faith, we can't pray effectively (Mark 11:22–24). The Word of God and prayer must always go together (Acts 6:4; John 15:7) lest our praying become zeal without knowledge. "I used to think I should close my Bible and pray for faith," said D. L. Moody, "but I came to see that it was in studying the Word that I was to get faith."

Habakkuk prayed because he was overwhelmed by God's splendor. "I stand in awe of your deeds" (Hab. 3:2 NIV). He had seen a vision of the greatness of God, recorded for us in verses 3–15, and this vision left him weak and helpless (v. 16). All he could do was cry out to God.

Many people have the idea that it's always an enjoyable experience getting to know God in a deeper way, but that's not what the saints of God in the Bible would say. Moses trembled at Mount Sinai when God gave the law (Heb. 12:18–21). Joshua fell on his face before the Lord (Josh. 5:13–15), as did David (1 Chron. 21:16). Daniel became exhausted and ill after seeing the visions God gave him (Dan. 8:27; 10:11). The vision of Christ's glory on the Mount of Transfiguration left Peter, James, and John facedown on the ground and filled with terror (Matt. 17:6). When John saw the glorified Christ, he fell at His feet as though dead (Rev. 1:17).

A plaque hanging in my study carries this quotation from A. W. Tozer: "To know God is at once the easiest and the most difficult thing in the world." God certainly has the ability to reveal Himself to us, for He can do anything; but it's a problem for God to find somebody who is ready to meet Him. God doesn't reveal Himself to superficial saints who are only looking for "a new experience" they can brag about, or to curious Christians who want to "sample" deeper fellowship with God but not at too great a price.

We are the ones who make it difficult to get to know God better. "Draw near to God and He will draw near to you" (James 4:8 NKJV). "But on this one will I look," says the Lord, "on him who is poor and of a contrite spirit, and who trembles at My word" (Isa. 66:2 NKJV). "My flesh trembles in fear of you," wrote the psalmist; "I stand in awe of your laws" (Ps. 119:120 NIV).

Habakkuk prayed because he wanted God's work to succeed. God had told him that He was "working a work" in the world (Hab. 1:5), and now the prophet prayed that God would keep that work alive and cause it to prosper. What God was doing wasn't the work Habakkuk would have chosen, but he accepted God's plan and prayed, "Thy will be done." When God revealed that work to Habakkuk, he cried out, "We shall not die" (v. 12). Then in 2:4, God told him that the only way to live was by faith. So, when Habakkuk prayed for God's work to stay alive, he was also praying that his own faith might grow.[2]

Finally, Habakkuk prayed because he wanted God to show mercy. The prophet agreed that the people of Judah deserved to be chastened, and that God's chastening would work out for their good, but he asked that God's heart of love would reveal itself in mercy. He was like Moses when he interceded for the nation at Mount Sinai (Ex. 32) and at Kadesh Barnea (Num. 14). Perhaps Habakkuk had the promise of Isaiah 54:7–8 in mind as he prayed (and see Jer. 10:23–24.). Certainly the Lord did show mercy to the Jews, for He preserved them in Babylon and then permitted a remnant to return to their land and establish the nation.

If, like Habakkuk, you ever become discouraged about the condition of the church, the state of the world, or your own spiritual life, take time to pray and seek God's mercy. Charles Spurgeon said, "Whether we like it or not, asking is the rule of the kingdom." The greatest need today is for intercessors. "And he saw that there was no man, and wondered that there was no intercessor" (Isa. 59:16).

VISION: PONDER THE GREATNESS OF GOD (3:3–15)

The Lord isn't likely to give us today a vision such as Habakkuk saw, but because it's recorded in the Word, we can ponder it and let the Spirit teach us from it.[3] God reveals His greatness in creation, in Scripture, and in history, and if we have eyes to see, we can behold His glory.[4]

God came in splendor (vv. 3–5). According to some scholars, Mount Paran is another name for the entire Sinai Peninsula, or for Mount Sinai itself (Deut. 33:2). Teman is usually identified with Edom. In this song, Habakkuk seems to be retracing the march of Israel from Sinai to the Promised Land.

Everything about this stanza reveals the glory of God. He is called "the Holy One" (Hab. 3:3; and see 1:12), a name used in Isaiah at least thirty times. "His glory covered the heavens" (3:3) is an anticipation of the time when His glory will cover all the earth (2:14). God's appearance was like the lightning that plays across the heavens before the storm breaks. All of creation joined in praising Him as "the earth was full of his praise." God's brightness was like the sunrise only to a greater degree (see Matt. 17:2). "Horns" means "rays": "Rays flashed from his hand" (Hab. 3:4 NIV) where His power was hidden.

Verse 5 takes us to Egypt, where God revealed His power and glory in the plagues and pestilences that devastated the land and took the lives of the firstborn (Ex. 7—12). Those ten plagues were not only punishment because of Pharaoh's hardness of heart; they also revealed the vanity of Egypt's gods. "Against all the gods of Egypt I will execute judgment: I am the Lord" (Ex. 12:12; see also Ps. 78:50). But this verse might also include the various judgments God sent to Israel when they disobeyed Him from time to time during their wilderness march.

In Old Testament times, God often revealed His glory through such judgments, but in this present dispensation, He reveals His glory through Jesus Christ. "And the Word became flesh and dwelt among us, and we beheld His glory, the glory as of the only begotten of the Father, full of grace and truth" (John 1:14 NKJV). Pharaoh wouldn't acknowledge the truth, so he couldn't experience the grace. The first plague of Moses in Egypt was the turning of water into blood (Ex. 7:14–25), while our Lord's first recorded miracle was the turning of water into wine.

The Lord stood in power (vv. 6–7). Invading generals either push forward to gain ground or they fall back in retreat, but the Lord simply stood and faced the enemy unafraid. In fact, He calmly measured the earth[5] as a sign that He possessed it. To measure something is an indication that it's yours, and you can do with it what you please. It's also a preliminary step to action, as though the Lord were surveying the situation and estimating how much power it would take to execute His wrath on the nations. The Lord revealed His power when He shook the earth at Sinai before He delivered His law to Israel (Ex. 19:18; Heb. 12:18–21).

The nations that lay between Egypt and Canaan are typified by Cushan and Midian, two peoples living near Edom. As the news of the exodus from Egypt spread quickly through the nations, the people were terribly frightened and wondered what would happen to them when Israel arrived on the scene (Ex. 15:14–16; 23:27; Deut. 2:25; Josh. 2:8–11).

God marched in victory (vv. 8–15). Habakkuk uses dynamic poetic imagery to describe Israel's march through the wilderness as they followed the Lord to the Promised Land and then claimed their inheritance. The Red Sea opened to let Israel out of Egypt, and the Jordan opened to let Israel into Canaan. The Egyptian chariots sank into the mud and their occupants were drowned, but God's chariots were chariots of salvation. Verse 9 pictures the various battles that the Israelites fought en route to Canaan, battles that the Lord won for them as they trusted Him and obeyed His commands.

In verse 10, we move into the Promised Land and see Israel conquering the enemy. God was in complete control of land and water and used His creation to defeat the Canaanites. Verse 10 describes the victory of Deborah and Barak over Sisera (Judg. 4—5), when a sudden rainstorm turned their battlefield into a swamp and left the enemy's chariots completely useless. In Habakkuk 3:11, we have the famous miracle of Joshua when the day was prolonged so Joshua would have more time for a total victory (Josh. 10:12–13). Leading His army, God marched through Canaan like a farmer threshing grain, and His people claimed their inheritance (Hab. 3:12).

Expositors aren't agreed as to what historical event is described in verses 13–15. This could be a picture of the nation's deliverance from Egypt, but if it is, Habakkuk should have mentioned it earlier. God's "anointed" would be the nation of Israel, for they were a holy people to the Lord (Ex. 19:5–8). Perhaps the prophet is referring to the various times God had to deliver His people, as recorded in the book of Judges, and the "anointed one" would then be the judges He raised up and used to bring deliverance (Judg. 2:10–19).

However, perhaps Habakkuk was looking ahead and describing the deliverance of God's people from the Babylonian captivity. God brought the Medes and Persians to crush Babylon and then to permit the Jews to return to their land (Ezra 1:1–4). The image of God stripping Babylon "from head to foot" (Hab. 3:13 NIV) parallels what Jeremiah prophesied in Jeremiah 50—51. Perhaps Habakkuk was looking both to the past (the exodus) and to the future (deliverance from Babylon) and using the ancient victory to encourage the people to expect a new victory.[6]

In this hymn, Habakkuk describes his God, the God of Abraham, Isaac, and Jacob, and the God and Father of our Lord Jesus Christ. He is the God of glory who reveals His glory in creation and in history. He is the living God who makes the dead idols of the nations look ridiculous. He is the God of power who can command land and sea, heaven, and earth, and therefore, He is the God of victory who leads His people in triumph.

There is no substitute for good theology, whether in our sermons or in our songs. The shallowness of some contemporary sermons, books, and songs may be the major contributing factor to the weakness of the church and the increase in "religious entertainment" in meetings where we ought to be praising God. The thing that lifted Habakkuk to the mountaintop was his understanding of the greatness of God. We need a return to the kind of worship that focuses on the glory of God and seeks to honor Him alone.[7]

FAITH: AFFIRM THE WILL OF GOD (3:16–19)

This is one of the greatest confessions of faith found anywhere in Scripture. Habakkuk has faced the frightening fact that his nation will be invaded by a merciless enemy. The prophet knows that many of the people will go into exile and many will be slain. The land will be ruined, and Jerusalem and the temple will be destroyed. Yet he tells God that he will trust Him no matter what happens! Listen to his confession of faith.

"I will wait patiently on the Lord" (see v. 16). If Habakkuk had depended on his feelings, he would never have made this great confession of faith. If Habakkuk looked ahead, he saw a nation heading for destruction, and that frightened him. When he looked within, he saw himself trembling with fear, and when he looked around, he saw everything in the economy about to fall apart. But when he looked up by faith, he saw God, and all his fears vanished. To walk by faith means to focus on the greatness and glory of God.

One of the marks of faith is a willingness to wait patiently for the Lord to work. "Whoever believes will not act hastily" (Isa. 28:16 NKJV). When we run ahead of God, we get into trouble. Abraham learned that lesson when he married Hagar and fathered Ishmael (Gen. 16), and so did Moses when he tried to deliver the Jews by his own hand (Ex. 2). "In quietness and confidence shall be your strength" (Isa. 30:15 NKJV).

Habakkuk could wait quietly because he knew that God was at work in the world (Hab. 1:5), and he had prayed that God's work would be kept alive and strong (3:2). When you know that God is working in your life, you can afford to wait quietly and let Him have His way. Furthermore, God had commanded him to wait (2:3), and "God's commandments are God's enablements." No matter what we see and no matter how we feel, we must depend on God's promises and not allow ourselves to "fall apart." "Rest in the Lord, and wait patiently for him" (Ps. 37:7).

Over the years, I've often leaned on three verses that have helped me wait patiently on the Lord. "Stand still" (Ex. 14:13), "Sit still" (Ruth 3:18), and "Be still" (Ps. 46:10). Whenever we find ourselves getting "churned up" within, we can be sure that we need to stop, pray, and wait on the Lord before we do some stupid thing.

"I will rejoice in the Lord" (vv. 17–18). By the time Babylon was through with the land of Judah, there wouldn't be much of value left (2:17). Buildings would be destroyed, treasures would be plundered, and farms and orchards would be devastated. The economy would fall apart and there would be little to sing about. But God would still be on His throne, working out His divine purposes for His people (Rom. 8:28).

Habakkuk couldn't rejoice in his circumstances, but he could rejoice in his God!

The prophet's testimony here reminds us of Paul's admonitions to Christians today: "Rejoice always, pray without ceasing, in everything give thanks; for this is the will of God in Christ Jesus for you" (1 Thess. 5:16–18 NKJV). Habakkuk discovered that God was his strength (Hab. 3:19) and song as well as his salvation (see Isa. 12:1–2; Ex. 15:2; Ps. 118:14); and therefore he had nothing to fear.

It's one thing to "whistle in the dark" and try to bolster our courage, and quite something else to sing about the eternal God who never fails. Though his lips were trembling and his legs were shaking (Hab. 3:16 NIV), the prophet burst into song and worshipped his God. What an example for us to follow! It reminds us of our Lord before He went to the cross (Mark 14:26), and Paul and Silas in the Philippian dungeon (Acts 16:19–34). God can give us "songs in the night" (Ps. 42:8; 77:6; Job 35:10) if we'll trust Him and see His greatness.

"I will rely on the Lord" (see v. 19). If my legs were shaking and my heart pounding, I'd find a safe place to sit down and relax, but Habakkuk began to bound up the mountain like a deer! Because of his faith in the Lord, he was able to stand and be as sure-footed as a deer; he was able to run swiftly and go higher than he'd ever gone before. This is one reason why the Lord permits us to go through trials: They can draw us nearer to Him and lift us above the circumstances so that we walk on the heights with Him.

God made us for the heights. If He allows us to go into the valley, it's so we might wait on Him and mount up with eagles' wings (Isa. 40:30–31). "He made him ride on the high places of the earth" (Deut. 32:13). This is what David experienced when he was being chased by his enemies and by Saul: "It is God who arms me with strength, and makes my way perfect. He makes my feet like the feet of deer, and sets me on my high places" (Ps. 18:32–33 NKJV).

The great British expositor G. Campbell Morgan said, "Our joy is in proportion to our trust. Our trust is in proportion to our knowledge of God."[8] The hymn "Joy and Peace in Believing" paraphrases Habakkuk 3:17–19:

> Though vine nor fig-tree neither
>> Their wonted fruit shall bear;
> Though all the fields should wither,
>> Nor flocks nor herds be there;
> Yet God the same abiding,
>> His praise shall tune my voice;
> For while in Him confiding,
>> I cannot but rejoice.

Habakkuk teaches us to face our doubts and questions honestly, take them humbly to the Lord, wait for His Word to teach us, and then worship Him no matter how we feel or what we see.

God doesn't always change the circumstances, but He can change us to meet the circumstances. That's what it means to live by faith.

QUESTIONS FOR PERSONAL REFLECTION
OR GROUP DISCUSSION

1. What is a current challenge in your life that requires faith?

2. Wiersbe says that Habakkuk "was living by promises, not explanations." Look back at 2:4, 14, 20. How were these promises more valuable than explanations? What promises are you living by?

3. Prayer, vision, and faith took Habakkuk from the valley to the summit. According to 3:2, why did Habakkuk pray?

4. What did he ask for?

5. How would you define or describe God's glory? How does Habakkuk portray God's glory in 3:3–15?

6. How do you respond to this picture of God?

7. How does God reveal His glory today? Talk about your own experience.

8. What does it mean to "walk by faith"? What are some marks of true faith?

9. Describe Habakkuk's emotions in 3:16 and the reason why he felt that way.

10. How easy is it for you to have faith and wait patiently when you're in a situation like that? What helps you?

11. How can we rejoice when circumstances are difficult? How can we help others who don't seem able to rejoice?

12. According to Wiersbe in the last two paragraphs of the chapter, what does Habakkuk teach us? What have you learned?

MALACHI IN HIS TIME

The name Malachi means "My messenger" (3:1). He was the last of the writing prophets but wrote nothing about himself. We have no biblical information about his ancestry, call, or personal life. But the important thing about messengers is the message they bring, not who they are or where they came from.

In 538 BC, Cyrus issued a decree that the Jews exiled in Babylon could return to their land and rebuild their temple (2 Chron. 36:22–23; Ezra 1). About fifty thousand of them accepted the challenge; and in 515, after much delay, they completed the temple. Ezra visited them in 458, and in 445 Nehemiah became their governor and served for twelve years (Neh. 5:14).

While Nehemiah was back at his post in Shushan (Neh. 13:6–7), things began to fall apart in Jerusalem, and when he returned, he had to take some drastic steps to reform the nation. It's possible that the prophet Malachi was called at that time to expose the sins of the people and call them back to God.

The conditions described in the book of Nehemiah are the very things Malachi deals with in his book: poor crops and a faltering economy (Mal. 3:11), intermarriage with the heathen (2:11), defilement of the priesthood

(1:6ff.), oppression of the poor (3:5), lack of support for the temple (vv. 8–10), and a general disdain of religion (v. 13ff.). It was a low time spiritually for Judah, and they needed to hear the Word of God.

Malachi was the last prophet Judah heard until John the Baptist came and the prophecy of 3:1 was fulfilled. His messages against "the sins of the saints" need to be heeded today.

A Suggested Outline of the Book of Malachi[1]

Theme: Honoring the name of God by living godly lives
Key verse: Malachi 1:11

I. Doubting God's Love (Malachi 1:1–5)
    1. God's electing grace (Malachi 1:2)
    2. God's blessing on Israel (Malachi 1:3–5)

II. Dishonoring God's Name (Malachi 1:6—2:9)
    1. Offering defiled sacrifices (Malachi 1:6–14)
    2. Despising divine privileges (Malachi 2:1–9)

III. Profaning God's Covenant (Malachi 2:10–16)
    1. Marrying heathen women (Malachi 2:10–12)
    2. Offering hypocritical repentance (Malachi 2:13)
    3. Divorcing their Jewish wives (Malachi 2:14–16)

IV. Questioning God's Justice (Malachi 2:17—3:6)
    1. Where are the promised blessings? (Malachi 2:17)
    2. The first messenger—John the Baptist (Malachi 3:1a)
    3. The second messenger—Messiah (Malachi 3:1b–6)

V. Robbing God's Storehouse (Malachi 3:7–12)
    1. Robbing God (Malachi 3:7–8)
    2. Robbing themselves (Malachi 3:9–11)
    3. Robbing others (Malachi 3:12)

VI. Despising God's Service (Malachi 3:13—4:6)
    1. The complainers (Malachi 3:13–15)
    2. The believers (Malachi 3:16–18)
    3. The evildoers (Malachi 4:1–3)
    4. The preachers (Malachi 4:4–6)

Chapter Twelve

THE SINS OF GOD'S PEOPLE—PART I

(Malachi 1—2:16)

A church member scolded her pastor for preaching a series of sermons on "The Sins of the Saints."

"After all," she argued, "the sins of Christians are different than the sins of other people."

"Yes," agreed her pastor, "they're worse."

They *are* worse, for when believers sin, they not only break the law of God, but they break the heart of God. When a believer deliberately sins, it isn't just the disobedience of a servant to a master, or the rebellion of a subject against a king; it's the offense of a child against the loving Father. The sins we cherish and think we can get away with bring grief to the heart of God.

Malachi was called to perform a difficult and dangerous task. It was his responsibility to rebuke the people for the sins they were committing against God and against one another, and to call them to return to the Lord. Malachi took a wise approach: He anticipated the objections of the people and met them head-on. "This is what God says," declared the prophet, "but you say __," and then he would answer their complaints. The Old Testament prophets were often the only people in the community who had a grip on reality and saw things as they actually were, and that's what made them so unpopular. "Prophets were twice stoned," said Christopher Morley, "first in anger, then, after their death, with a handsome slab in the graveyard."

In this chapter, we'll study what Malachi wrote concerning three of their sins, and then we'll consider the remaining three in the next chapter. But don't read Malachi as ancient history. Unfortunately, these sins are with us in the church today.

DOUBTING GOD'S LOVE (1:1–5)

Like Nahum (1:1) and Habakkuk (1:1), Malachi called his message a "burden." The prophets were men who personally felt "the burden of the Lord" as God gave them insight into the hearts of the people and the problems of society. It wasn't easy for Malachi to strip the veneer off the piety of the priests and expose their hypocrisy, or to repeat to the people the complaints they were secretly voicing against the Lord, but that's what God called him to do. "The task of a prophet," writes Eugene Peterson, "is not to smooth things over but to make things right."[1]

The first sin Malachi named was the people's lack of love for God. That was the first sin Jesus mentioned when He wrote to the seven churches of Asia Minor (Rev. 2:4), and perhaps it's listed first because lack of love for God is the source of all other sin. For centuries, the Jews have recited the "Shema"[2] as their daily prayer: "Hear, O Israel: The Lord our God, the Lord is one! You shall love the Lord your God with all your heart, with all your soul, and with all your strength" (Deut. 6:4–5 NKJV). But the people Malachi preached to doubted that God even loved them, so why should they love Him?

The prophet presented several evidences of God's love for Israel, the first of which is God's clear statement of His love (Mal. 1:2a). Malachi was probably referring to what the Lord said through Moses in the book of Deuteronomy, particularly 7:6–11. When God gave the law at Sinai, the emphasis was, "Obey My law because I am a holy God." But when Moses reviewed the law for the new generation, the emphasis was, "Obey the Lord because He loves you and you love Him." Both motives are valid today.

The second evidence of God's love that Malachi presented was God's electing grace (Mal. 1:2b–3). As the firstborn in the family, Esau should have inherited both the blessing and the birthright, but the Lord gave them to his younger brother Jacob (Gen. 25:21–23).[3] The descendants of Esau had their land assigned to them, but God gave the Edomites no covenants of blessing as He did to Jacob's descendants.

The statement that God loved Jacob but hated Esau has troubled some people. Paul quoted it in Romans 9:10–13 to prove God's electing grace for both Israel and all who trust Jesus Christ for salvation. But the verb "hate" must not be defined as a positive expression of the wrath of God. God's love for Jacob was so great that, in comparison, His actions toward Esau looked like hatred. As an illustration, Jacob loved Rachel so much that his relationship to Leah seemed like hatred (Gen. 29:20, 30–31; see also Deut. 21:15–17). When Jesus called His disciples to "hate" their own family (Luke 14:26), He was using the word *hate* in a similar way. Our love for Christ may occasionally move us to do things that appear like hatred to those whom we love (see Matt. 12:46–50).

Someone said to Dr. Arno C. Gaebelein, the gifted Hebrew Christian leader of a generation ago, "I have a serious problem with Malachi 1:3, where God says, 'Esau I have hated.'" Dr. Gaebelein replied, "I have a greater problem with Malachi 1:2, where God says, 'Jacob, I have loved.'" We certainly can't explain the love and grace of God, nor do we have to, but we can experience God's grace and love as we trust Christ and walk with Him. The Lord is even willing to be "the God of Jacob."

Malachi's third evidence for God's love is God's evident blessing on the people of Israel (v. 4). Like other nations in that area, Edom suffered during the Babylonian invasion of Israel, but the Lord didn't promise to restore their land as He promised the Jews. The proud Edomites boasted that they would quickly have their land in good shape, but God had other plans. He called Edom "The Wicked Land" (v. 4 NIV), but Israel He called "the holy land" (Zech. 2:12).⁴ Keep in mind that the Edomites were indeed an evil people (see Obad. 8–14) who deserved every judgment God sent their way. To the Jews, the Babylonian invasion was a chastening, but to Edom, it was a judgment.

Think of how God showed His love to the Jewish people. First, He spared the Jews who were in exile in Babylon (see Jer. 29). Then, He moved Cyrus to issue the decree that enabled the Jews to return to Judah and rebuild the temple. He provided the leadership of Joshua the high priest, Zerubbabel, Nehemiah, and Ezra, as well as the prophetic ministry of Haggai, Zechariah, and Malachi. Had His people obeyed the terms of the covenant, the Lord would have blessed them even more. Yes, they were a weak remnant, but the Lord was with them and promised to bless them.

Note that the name God uses in Malachi 1:4 is "Lord of hosts" ("Lord Almighty" in the NIV), that is, "the Lord of the armies," a name used twenty-four times in Malachi and nearly three hundred times in the Old Testament. This is the "military" name of God, for "hosts" comes from a Hebrew word that means "to wage war." The Lord is the Commander of the hosts and heaven: the stars (Isa. 40:26; Gen. 2:1), the angels (Ps. 103:20–21), the armies of Israel (Ex. 12:41), and all who trust in Him (Ps. 46:7, 11).

Finally, Malachi reminded the Jews of the great privilege God gave them to witness to the Gentiles (Mal. 1:5). During the reigns of David and Solomon, God manifested His glory through the nation of Israel so that the Gentiles came from distant lands to see what was happening in Israel. To a lesser degree, this also happened during the times of Josiah and Hezekiah. But the destruction of Jerusalem and the temple gave the

Gentiles opportunity to ridicule Israel and laugh at their religion and their God (Ps. 74; 137; Jer. 18:13–17; Lam. 2:15–16).

When God brought His remnant back to the land, He wanted to bless them and once again manifest His glory through them, but they failed to trust Him and obey His law. Though they had been chastened by God and ruined by Babylon, and though they had lost the esteem of the Gentile nations around them, the Jews could have made a new beginning and witnessed to the Gentiles of the grace and mercy of God. Instead, they lapsed into the sins that Malachi attacks in his book, and they gave but a weak witness to the other nations. They missed their opportunity to glorify God.

But we need to remind ourselves that the trials we experience as individuals or congregations are also opportunities to glorify God before a watching world. That's how Paul viewed his imprisonment and possible death in Rome (Phil. 1:12–26), and that's the way we must look at the testings God sends our way. Every difficulty is an opportunity to demonstrate to others what the Lord can do for those who put their trust in Him.

DISHONORING GOD'S NAME (1:6—2:9)

Now Malachi directs his message especially to the priests (1:6; 2:1, 7–8), who, instead of living exemplary lives, were guilty of breaking the very law they were supposed to obey and teach. The way they were serving the Lord was a disgrace to His name.

Eight times in this section you find the phrase "my name" (1:6, 11, 14; 2:2, 5; see also 3:16 and 4:2), referring, of course, to God's character and reputation. The priests who were supposed to honor God's name were disgracing it before the people and the Lord. The priests were supposed to be God's children, yet they weren't honoring their Father; they were called to be God's servants, yet they showed no respect for their Master. When

Malachi confronted them, the priests arrogantly asked, "In what way have we despised Your name?" (1:6 NKJV), so he told them.

To begin with, they were offering defiled sacrifices on the altar (vv. 6–14). The word *bread* means "food" and refers to the sacrifices provided in the law of Moses (Lev. 1—7). These animals had to be perfect; nothing imperfect could be brought to the altar of God and accepted (Deut. 15:19–23; Lev. 22:17–33). After all, these sacrifices pointed to the Lamb of God who would one day die for the sins of the world (John 1:29; Heb. 10:1–14), and if they were imperfect, how could they typify the Perfect Sacrifice, the Son of God?

In short, the priests were permitting the people to bring God less than their best. If they had offered these defective beasts to their governor, he would have rejected them, but the animals were good enough for the Lord. These priests had forgotten what was written in their own law: "Do not bring anything with a defect, because it will not be accepted on your behalf" (Lev. 22:20 NIV). What does this say to professed Christians who spend hundreds of dollars annually, perhaps thousands, on gifts for themselves, their family, and their friends, but give God a dollar a week when the offering plate is passed?

Our offerings to God are an indication of what's in our hearts, "for where your treasure is, there will your heart be also" (Matt. 6:21). People who claim to love the Lord and His work can easily prove it with their checkbooks! Giving is a grace (2 Cor. 8:1, 6–9), and if we've experienced the grace of God, we'll have no problem giving generously to the Lord who has given so much to us. How can we ask God to be gracious to us and answer prayer (Mal. 1:9) if we've not practiced "grace giving" ourselves?

Malachi told these disobedient priests that it would be better to close the doors of the temple and stop the sacrifices altogether than to continue practicing such hypocrisy. Better there were no religion at all than a religion that fails to give God the very best. If our concept of God is so low that we think He's pleased with cheap, halfhearted worship, then we don't know the God of the Bible. In fact, a God who encourages us to do less than our best is a God who isn't worthy of worship.

The day will come when the Gentiles will worship God and magnify His great name (v. 11). Malachi looked ahead to the time when the message of salvation would be taken to all nations, and beyond that, he saw the establishing of the kingdom on earth when the Gentiles would "flow unto it" (Isa. 2:2; see also 11:3–4, 9; 45:22–25; 49:5–7). God's call to Abraham involved the Jews becoming a blessing to the whole earth (Gen. 12:1–3), just as His call to the church involves taking the gospel to all nations (Mark 16:15).

The priests even allowed the people to cheat on their vows (Mal. 1:13–14). If a man promised God a sacrifice but brought an animal that was sick or blemished, the priest would accept it, even though the man had a perfect animal back home. In the Mosaic law, vows were purely voluntary, but once they were made, they were binding (Lev. 27; Num. 30; Deut. 23:21–23). If the governor wouldn't accept cheap offerings (Mal. 1:8), would a great king accept cheap substitutes (v. 14)? God is a great King and He deserves the best we can bring Him. What we promise, we must perform.

Why did the priests deliberately disobey their own law, pollute the altar of the Lord, and encourage the people to worship God in a cheap, careless manner? For one thing, the priests themselves weren't giving God their best, so why make greater demands on the people? "Like people, like priest" (Hos. 4:9; see Jer. 5:30–31), for no ministry rises any higher than its leaders.

But there was another reason why blemished sacrifices were acceptable: The priests and their families were fed from the meat off the altar, and the priests wanted to be sure they had food on the table. After all, the economy was bad, taxes were high, and money was scarce, and only the most devoted Israelite would bring a perfect animal to the Lord. So the priests settled for less than the best and encouraged the people to bring whatever was available. A sick animal would die anyway, and crippled animals were useless, so the people might as well give them to the Lord! They forgot that "to obey is better than sacrifice, and to hearken than the fat of rams" (1 Sam. 15:22; Ps. 51:16–17; Mic. 6:6–8; Mark 12:28–34).

The priests dishonored God's name in another way: They despised the very privilege of being priests (Mal. 2:1–5). They were taking for granted the high calling God had given them and treating the temple ministry with contempt. Serving at the altar was a job, not a ministry, and they did it to please themselves, not to please and glorify the Lord. Unfortunately, that same attitude is in the church today.

God warned them that He would "curse their [Israel's] blessings" if they didn't start "doing the will of God from the heart" (Eph. 6:6) and giving Him their best. In fact, their crops had already been ruined by devouring insects (Mal. 3:11; see Hag. 1:3–11), but things could get worse. God warned that He could curse the very seed that was planted so that it would never germinate and produce a harvest. Since the law gave the priests and Levites a tithe of the produce, ruined crops would mean empty tables.

It's possible that the word *seed* in Malachi 2:3 may refer to their children. It was important that the Jews have children in order to perpetuate the nation, but God could prevent even the human seed from being productive. Another way of looking at it is that God would turn their children, who should be a blessing (Ps. 127), into a burden and a curse. It would be painful not to have children, but it would also be painful to have children who daily broke your heart and created grief in the home.

The refuse from the sacrifices was taken outside the camp and burned (Ex. 29:14), but God would humiliate the priests and "wipe their noses" in the dung of the sacrifices! This would make the priests unclean so that they would have to leave the camp. In short, God was saying, "You're treating Me with disrespect, so I'll treat you like garbage! You don't value the priestly ministry, so why should you be in office?"

The priests took their privileges for granted and forgot the gracious covenant God had made with them through Aaron (Mal. 2:4; Ex. 29) and Aaron's grandson Phinehas (Num. 25:1–13). It was a great privilege to be a priest, to serve at the altar, to minister in the temple, and to teach the law to the people. But the priests had no fear of God; they treated the sacred things as if they were common things because their hearts weren't right with God (Ezek. 44:23). The Scottish novelist George MacDonald said, "Nothing is so deadening to the divine as an habitual dealing with the outside of spiritual things." What the priests were doing wasn't ministry; it was only ritual, empty religious formality that disgusted the Lord.

There was a third sin: They turned away from God's law (Mal. 2:6–9). Verses 6–7 describe the perfect servants of God: truth on their lips, obedience in their walk, fellowship with God, a burden to bring others to the Lord, and a passion to share God's Word with those who need to hear it. But the priests weren't following this pattern; they were following their own ways. "They shall teach Jacob thy judgments, and Israel thy Law" (Deut. 33:10), but the priests weren't even obeying the law themselves. "The prophets prophesy falsely, and the priests rule by their own power; and My people love to have it so. But what will you do in the end?" (Jer. 5:31 NKJV).

It was bad enough that the priests were disobeying the law, but they were causing others to stumble as well (Mal. 2:8). Like the Pharisees Jesus described, the priests were "toxic" and defiled everything and everybody they touched (Matt. 23:15; 25–28). A false minister is an awful weapon in the hands of Satan. "One sinner destroys much good" (Eccl. 9:18 NIV). Because they showed partiality in the way they applied God's truth (Mal. 2:9), they disobeyed God and harmed His people. (See Lev. 19:15; Deut. 24:17; 1 Tim. 5:21.)

Over the years, I've participated in many ordination examinations, and I've looked for four characteristics in each candidate: a personal experience of salvation through faith in Jesus Christ; a sense of calling from the Lord; a love for and knowledge of the Word of God; and a high respect for the work of the ministry. Whenever we've examined a candidate who was flippant about ministry, who saw it as a job and not a divine calling, he didn't get my vote. Whether as a pastor, missionary, teacher, choir member, or usher, being a servant of God is a serious thing, and it deserves the very best that we can give.

God caused these hypocritical priests to be "despised and humiliated before all the people" (Mal. 2:9 NIV). The priests wanted to be popular, and even twisted the law to gain friends, but the people had no respect for them. Leaders with integrity and character will have their enemies, but they will still gain the respect of the people. The recent religious television scandals in America have proved that unsaved people expect church leaders to practice what they preach.

PROFANING GOD'S COVENANT (2:10–16)

Having dealt with the sins of the priests, Malachi now turns to the nation as a whole and confronts the men who divorced their wives to marry pagan women.

Treachery (vv. 10–11, 14). The men loving pagan women wasn't a new problem in the Jewish nation. When the Jews left Egypt, there was a "mixed multitude" that left with them (Ex. 12:38), which suggests that some Jews had married Egyptian spouses (Lev. 24:10; Num. 11:4). The Jews sinned greatly when they mixed with the women of Midian at Baal Peor (Num. 25), and God judged them severely. Ezra (Ezra 9:1–4) and Nehemiah (Neh. 13:23–31) had to contend with this problem, and it's not totally absent from the church today (2 Cor. 6:14–18).

In divorcing their Jewish wives and marrying pagan women, the men were committing several sins. To begin with, it was treachery as they broke their vows to God and to their wives. They were profaning God's covenant and treating it as nothing. Not only had the Lord given specific requirements for marriage in His law (Ex. 34:11–16; Deut. 7:3–4), but the covenant of marriage was built into creation. "Have we not all one father?" (Mal. 2:10) refers to God as the Father of all humans, the Creator (Acts. 17:28). God made men and women for each other and established marriage for the good of the human family. So, what these men did was contrary to what God had written into nature and in His covenant.

Hypocrisy (vv. 12–13). After committing these sins, the men then brought offerings to the Lord and wept at the altar (vv. 12–13), seeking His help and blessing. Perhaps they had the idea that they could sin blatantly with the intention of coming to God for forgiveness. But if they were truly repentant, they would have forsaken their heathen wives and taken their true wives back, which is what Ezra made them do (Ezra 9—10). These men were guilty of hypocritical worship that had nothing to do with a changed heart. Instead of forgiving them, God was ready to "cut them off."

In matters of ethics and morals, there are many things in society that are legal but are not biblical. Brides and grooms must remember that God is an unseen witness at every wedding (Mal. 2:14), and He also witnesses those who live together who aren't married. One day there will come a terrible harvest from the seeds being planted today by those who despise God's laws and the principles He has built into nature.

Purity (v. 15). In the entire book of Malachi, this is recognized as the most difficult verse to translate and interpret. I think the best translation is given by Dr. Gleason Archer: "But no one has done so who has a residue of the Spirit. And what does that one seek for? A godly offspring! Therefore take heed to your spirit [as a true believer under the covenant] and let none of you deal faithlessly with the wife of his youth."[5]

Here Malachi commended the faithful husbands who obeyed the Spirit of God and the Word of God. Unlike the men who took pagan wives just to satisfy their sexual hunger, these faithful men wanted to father children who would be a godly seed, devoted Jews, and not idol worshippers. The basic issue was not race, for humans are humans whether they are Jews or Midianites. The basic issue was loyalty to the God of Israel and the maintaining of a godly home.

God called Israel to be the channel for bringing the Messiah into the world, and anything that corrupted that stream would work against His great plan of salvation. God commanded the Jews to be a separate people, not because they were better than any other nation, but because He had a very special task for them to perform. Anything that broke down that wall of separation would play into the hands of the Evil One, who did all he could to keep the Messiah from being born.

Hostility (v. 16). "I hate divorce!" (NIV) is about as clear a statement as God can make.[6] Those who want to please God certainly wouldn't want to do anything that God so abhors, but would do everything possible to heal the marriage. God gave Adam one wife, not many, and He declared that the two were one flesh (Gen. 2:21–25). Divorce pulls apart that which God put together, and Jesus warned us not to do that (Matt. 19:6).[7] It's like an act of violence in an area where there ought to be tenderness.

Why does Malachi mention a "garment" and "violence"? In modern Western society, a man puts an engagement ring on a woman's finger to propose marriage, but in ancient Israel, he placed a corner of his garment over her (Ezek. 16:8; Ruth 3:9).[8] If a man divorces his wife, instead of having a garment that symbolized love, he had a garment that symbolized violence. He wrenched apart that which God said is one; by his infidelity, he made the marriage bed a place of violence.

In spite of a difficult text and differing interpretations, the main lessons of this passage are clear. In marriage, a man and a woman become one flesh, and God is a partner in that union. Through marriage, the Lord is seeking a godly seed that will carry on His work on earth. Marriage is a physical union ("one flesh") and can be broken by physical causes: death (Rom. 7:1–3), sexual sin (Matt. 19:9), or desertion (1 Cor. 7:12–16). God's original intent was that one man and one woman be devoted to each other in marriage for one lifetime. Divorce for reasons other than those given in Scripture, even though legal, would grieve the heart of God.

In its "Universal Declaration of Human Rights," the United Nations describes the family as "the natural and fundamental unit of society." Historians Will and Ariel Durant call the family "the nucleus of civilization." Strong families begin with strong marriages, a man and a woman who love each other and want to live each for the other and both for the Lord. Anything less than that is less than God's will.

QUESTIONS FOR PERSONAL REFLECTION
OR GROUP DISCUSSION

1. Why does Wiersbe think the sins of Christians are worse than those of non-Christians? What do you think about that?

2. "'The task of a prophet,' writes Eugene Peterson, 'is not to smooth things over but to make things right.'" Is this a task that comes easily to you? Explain.

3. Malachi said the people should love God because He loved them (1:2) and because he had chosen them to be His own people (1:2b–5). Why should we today love God?

4. God's love for Jacob was so great that, in comparison, His actions toward Esau looked like hatred. Does that seemingly unfairness bother you? Explain.

5. Malachi says that both Israel's blessings and her trials were opportunities to glorify God (1:5). How can trials be an opportunity to glorify God?

6. Why should we bring God our best (1:6, 14)?

7. How can we make sure to bring God our best?

8. What are some qualities of a great servant of God (2:6–7)?

9. Wiersbe thinks every ministry candidate, whether layperson or pastor, should have a high respect for the work of the ministry. Why is that so important?

10. What sins were the men committing when they divorced their Jewish wives and married pagan women? According to Wiersbe, what are the main lessons from the section on divorce?

11. What were the basic issues concerning God's displeasure at the mixed marriages? How did "race" fit in?

Chapter Thirteen

THE SINS OF GOD'S PEOPLE—PART II

(Malachi 2:17—4:6)

As Malachi continued his message, the people continued their resistance to God's truth. They had already argued with him about God's love (1:2), God's name (v. 6), and God's teaching about marriage and divorce (2:14), and now they would argue about three other matters: the justice of God, giving to God, and serving God. People who argue with God rarely receive blessings from God. It's when our mouth is stopped and we submit to His will that we can experience the grace of God (Rom. 3:19).

But Malachi didn't stop preaching; he went on to deal with these "sins of the saints."

QUESTIONING GOD'S JUSTICE (2:17—3:6)

"You have wearied the Lord with your words," the prophet said; and they replied, "How have we wearied Him?" (2:17 NIV). Of course, God never gets weary in a physical sense because God doesn't have a body (Isa. 40:28), but He does grow weary of some of the things His people say and do. The hypocritical people in Israel wearied God with their iniquities (43:24), and the Jewish remnant in Malachi's day wearied Him with their words.

Their words were cynical and skeptical. "We came back to the land, rebuilt the temple, and restored the worship," they said, "and look at the difficulties we're experiencing! Why isn't God keeping His promise? Where are all the blessings He promised through His prophets?" It was the age-old problem of "Why do the righteous suffer while the wicked prosper?" Job and his friends wrestled with it, and so did Asaph (Ps. 73), Jeremiah (Jer. 12), and Habakkuk.

But these skeptical Jews had forgotten the terms of the covenant and the conditions laid down by the prophets: If the people obeyed God's law, God would bless them with all they needed. But they were divorcing their wives, marrying pagan women, offering defiled sacrifices, robbing God of tithes and offerings, and complaining about having to serve the Lord! For God to bless people like that would mean approving of their sins. The Jews didn't need justice; they needed mercy!

Malachi answered their question "Where is the God of justice?" by speaking about two messengers.

"My messenger"—John the Baptist (v. 1a). As we've seen, the name Malachi means "my messenger"; and the messenger referred to in this statement we know as John the Baptist. Speaking of John the Baptist, Jesus said, "For this is he of whom it is written, 'Behold, I send My messenger before Your face who will prepare Your way before You'" (Matt. 11:10 NKJV; see Mark 1:2 and Luke 7:27).

While Malachi was the last of the writing prophets, John the Baptist was the last and the greatest of the old covenant prophets.[1] To John was given the unique privilege of ministering at the close of the old dispensation and the beginning of the new, and it was John who presented Jesus to Israel (John 1:29–31). Like Jeremiah and Ezekiel, John was born into a priestly family but was called of God to be a prophet. He was also a martyr, for he gave his life in the work God called him to do (Matt. 14:1–12).

The prophet Isaiah had also written about John's ministry (Isa. 40:3–5;

Mark 1:3; Luke 3:4–6; John 1:23). The image is that of people preparing a way for the king to come, leveling the roads and removing the obstacles so that the king might enjoy an easy and comfortable trip. John prepared the way for the ministry of Jesus by preaching the Word to the crowds, urging them to repent of their sins, baptizing them, and then introducing them to Jesus.

But how does this answer the question "Where is God's justice for His people?" When Jesus Christ came and died on the cross, He completely satisfied the justice of God. He paid the penalty for the sins of the world and vindicated the holiness of God. Nobody can ever truthfully say, "God isn't just!" The cross of Christ is proof that the same God who ordained "the law of sin and death" (Gen. 2:15–17; Rom. 6:23; 8:2–4) also "took His own medicine" (to quote Dorothy Sayers) and willingly died for sinners. Because of Calvary, God is both "just and justifier" of all who trust Jesus Christ (3:26).

"The Messenger of the covenant"—Jesus Christ (3:1b–6). The first prophecy refers to our Lord's first coming in grace and mercy, but this prophecy speaks of His second coming in judgment. When He comes, He will prove that God is just by purifying His people and judging rebellious sinners. Jesus Christ is the "Messenger of the covenant" in that He fulfilled all the demands of the covenant in His life, suffered the penalties in His death, and rose from the dead to usher in a new covenant of grace (Jer. 31:31–40; Matt. 26:26–30; Heb. 8:6–13). All the covenants in Old Testament history unite in pointing to Jesus Christ and His marvelous work of redemption.

An unannounced coming (3:3). Messiah's second coming will be sudden and unexpected, and its purpose will be the judging of sinners and the establishing of His kingdom on earth. "But of that day and hour no one knows, not even the angels of heaven, but My Father only" (Matt. 24:36 NKJV). "For when they say, 'Peace and safety!' then sudden destruction comes upon them, as labor pains upon a pregnant woman" (1 Thess. 5:3 NKJV).

An unprepared people (3:1). The phrase "whom ye delight in" suggests that the Jews in Malachi's day were hoping that "the day of the Lord" would come soon, not realizing what a terrible day it would be for the whole earth. His listeners were like the people in the days of Amos, the prophet who had the same false confidence that they were ready for the promised "day of the Lord." Amos warned them, "Woe to you who long for the day of the Lord! Why do you long for the Day of the Lord? That day will be darkness, not light" (Amos 5:18 NIV; and see vv. 19–20).

When the Jewish remnant of that day read the prophets, they saw only the promises of blessing and not the warnings of judgment. They rejoiced in the prophecies of the coming King and His glorious kingdom, but they overlooked the prophecies that described worldwide terror when the wrath of God is poured out on sinners.[2] These Israelites were not unlike some Christians today who talk about the coming of the Lord as though seeing Him will be more like beholding a visiting celebrity and basking in his or her glory. Standing at the judgment seat of Christ will be an awesome experience, even though we know that we have a place reserved for us in heaven.

An unclean nation (3:2–4). Malachi asked, "But who may abide the day of his coming?" and then described what Messiah would do when He came: He would purify the Jewish nation, especially the priests, and bring swift judgment to the sinners who arrogantly disobeyed His law.

In the law of Moses, God provided three ways for people and things to be cleansed and made acceptable to God: water, fire, and blood. There is no mention here of blood because Jesus Christ died for sinners at His first coming. But He would wash the unclean nation like a launderer washes dirty clothes. He would purify the tribe of Levi the way a jeweler purifies precious metal in his furnace. "In that day there shall be a fountain opened to the house of David and to the inhabitants of Jerusalem for sin and for uncleanness" (Zech. 13:1).

Once the nation is cleansed and the priests are purified, then they can become an acceptable sacrifice to the Lord (Mal. 3:4), and He will be pleased with them. The priests in Malachi's time were offering sacrifices that were unacceptable (1:7–8), and the priests themselves were unacceptable, but in that great day, God's Messenger would make His people "living sacrifices" that would be acceptable to the Lord (Rom. 12:1).

An unsparing judgment (3:5). This list of sinners gives us some idea of the kind of practices that were going on in Malachi's time and will be going on in the end times. All of them are contrary to God's law. Sorcery is forbidden because it means trafficking with demons (Ex. 22:18; Lev. 20:27; Deut. 18:14). The "satanic revival" that's going on today indicates that many people aren't heeding God's warnings as they dabble in witchcraft and other demonic practices. In fact, witchcraft is a legal religion in many places.

As for adulterers, we've already heard Malachi's message to the men who divorced their Jewish wives to marry pagan women. "Thou shalt not commit adultery" (Ex. 20:14) is still in the Bible no matter what the marriage laws permit.

"False swearers" describes people who commit perjury by lying while under oath. Perjury violates the third commandment, "Thou shalt not take the name of the Lord thy God in vain" (v. 7), and the ninth commandment, "Thou shalt not bear false witness against thy neighbor" (v. 16). Trust is the "cement" that holds society together, and when that cement crumbles, society falls apart. If we can't trust one another's words and promises, then how can we live and work together safely?

The oppressing of the poor and needy is a sin that the prophets condemned with vehemence, and it needs to be condemned today. God has a special concern for widows and orphans who are exploited and laborers who don't receive their wages (Ex. 22:22–24; Lev. 19:10; Deut. 10:17–19; 24:14–15, 19–22; 27:19; Ps. 68:5; Isa. 1:17, 23: Jer. 7:6; James 5:1–8).

An unchanging God (3:6). What was the reason for these social abuses? The people who committed them had no fear of the Lord. They thought that God was like themselves, that He would close His eyes to their sins and not judge them for breaking His law. "You thought that I was altogether like you; but I will rebuke you" (Ps. 50:21 NKJV).

The Jews should have been grateful that God was unchanging in His nature, His purposes, and His promises, for if He were not, He would have consumed them for their sins. Twice Moses used this truth about God as his argument when he interceded for the nation (Ex. 33:12–23; Num. 14:11–21). The same principle applies to believers today, for 1 John 1:9 states that God is "faithful and just to forgive our sins." God is faithful to His promises and just toward His Son who died for our sins that we might be forgiven. (See also Num. 23:19; Deut. 4:31; James 1:17.)

Malachi has proved that God is just. Now he discusses the fact that the people are unjust in the way they've robbed God of what rightfully belongs to Him.

ROBBING GOD'S STOREHOUSE (3:7–12)

If "like people, like priest" (Hos. 4:9) applied to the spiritual leaders of the nation, then "like father, like son" (or "like mother, like daughter") applied to everybody else. From the days of the patriarchs until Malachi's time, the nation frequently disobeyed God's Word, and God had to send prophets to call them to repent and return.

When the people heard Malachi call them to return to the Lord, instead of obeying that call, they began to argue with God's servant. They remind me of those people who evade the issue by saying, "Define your terms! What do you mean by 'return'?" But Malachi didn't hesitate to tell them how to start returning to God: "Bring God the tithes and offerings that are rightfully His!" Theirs was the sin of robbery in at least three different areas.

(1) They were robbing God (vv. 7–8). The needs of the priests and Levites were met from the sacrifices and also from the tithes and offerings brought to the temple by the people. The word *tithe* comes from a Hebrew word that means "ten." A tithe is 10 percent of one's grain, fruit, animals, or money (Lev. 27:30–34; Neh. 13:5). There were special storage rooms in the temple for keeping the grain, produce, and money that the people brought to the Lord in obedience to His law. If people didn't want to carry heavy produce all the way to the temple, they could convert it into cash, but they had to add 20 percent to it just to make sure they weren't making a profit and robbing God (Lev. 27:31).

The annual tithe was given to the Levites (Num. 18:21–24), who in turn gave a tithe of that income to the priests (vv. 25–32). When a worshipper brought his tithe to the temple, he could use part of it to enjoy a special meal with his family and the Levites (Deut. 12:6–7, 17–19). Every third year a tithe was to be brought to the leaders locally to be used for the poor (14:28–29).

Tithing as an act of worship is as old as Abraham, who gave tithes to Melchizedek, acknowledging that Melchizedek was the representative of the Most High God (Gen. 14:20; Heb. 7). Jacob vowed to God that he would tithe (Gen. 28:22), so tithing antedates the law of Moses. However, tithing was officially incorporated into the law of Moses as a part of Israel's worship. In bringing the tithes and offerings, the people were not only supporting the ministry of the temple, but they were also giving thanks to God for His bountiful provision for their own needs.

Over the centuries, many of the Jews committed two errors with regard to the tithe: (1) the legalists obeyed the law so scrupulously that, like the Pharisees, they even tithed the minute garden herbs (Matt. 23:23–24), all the while thinking that their obedience would earn them righteousness before God; (2) the irreligious neglected the tithe and by disobeying God deprived the temple ministry of what it needed to keep going. When Nehemiah returned to Jerusalem, the temple storerooms were empty of produce and many of the priests and Levites had abandoned their service to go back home and work their fields in order to care for their families (Neh. 13:10). The people had vowed to bring their tithes (10:34–39), but they hadn't kept their vow.

Since God made and owns everything, He doesn't need anything that we can bring Him (Acts 17:25). But when we obey His Word and bring our gifts as an act of worship with grateful hearts, it pleases Him. While 1 Corinthians 16:1–2 suggests proportionate giving ("as God has prospered him"),[3] there is no express command to tithe given to the church in the New Testament. Paul teaches "grace giving" in 2 Corinthians 8—9, which is certainly beyond 10 percent. Many Christians feel that if believers under the old covenant brought their tithes, how could Christians under the new covenant begin with anything less?

(2) They were robbing themselves (vv. 9–11). In robbing God, the people were not fulfilling the covenant they had made with the Lord; therefore, God couldn't fulfill His promise and bless them (Lev. 26:3ff.). "The Lord will command the blessing on you in your storehouses and in all to which you set your hand, and He will bless you in the land" (Deut. 28:8 NKJV). Insects had invaded the land ("the devourer," Mal. 3:11) and the grain and fruit were not maturing.

Whenever we rob God, we always rob ourselves. To begin with, we rob ourselves of the spiritual blessings that always accompany obedience and faithful giving (2 Cor. 9:6–15). But even more, the money that rightfully belongs to God that we keep for ourselves never stays with us. It ends up going to the doctor, the auto body shop, or the tax collector. "You have sown much, and bring in little … and he who earns wages, earns wages to put into a bag with holes" (Hag. 1:6 NKJV). If we don't trust God to care for us, whatever we do trust will prove futile. People who lovingly give tithes and offerings to God find that whatever is left over goes much further and brings much greater blessing.

Yes, giving is an act of faith, but God rewards that faith in every way. That isn't the reason we give, because that kind of motivation would be selfish. "If you give because it pays, it won't pay!" said industrialist R. G. LeTourneau, and he was right. We give because we love God and want to obey Him, and because He's very generous to us. When we lay up treasures in heaven, they pay rich dividends for all eternity.

The promise in Malachi 3:10 was linked to the covenant the Israelites had made with the Lord (Deut. 28:1–14), so if they faithfully obeyed Him, He would faithfully keep His promises. But the spiritual principle behind this promise is echoed in Luke 6:38 and 2 Corinthians 9:6–8, so believers today can lay hold of it. For some Christians in America, a tithe would be much too small an amount, but each believer must be fully persuaded in his or her heart what the Lord wants him or her to do.[4]

(3) They were robbing others (v. 12). The remnant that returned to Judah after the exile had a great opportunity to trust God and bear witness to the other nations that their God was the true and living God. Had the Jews trusted the Lord, He would have done great things for them, and they would have been a testimony to others. As it was, they floundered in their faith and nobody could look at them and call them blessed.

God's promise was, "The Lord will establish you as a holy people to Himself, just as He has sworn to you, if you keep the commandments of the Lord your God and walk in His ways. Then all the peoples of the earth shall see that you are called by the name of the Lord, and they shall be afraid of you" (Deut. 28:9–10 NKJV). The Gentiles would have come to Jerusalem to learn about this great and wonderful God who could take a group of refugees and turn them into a blessed nation.

DESPISING GOD'S SERVICE (3:13—4:6)

This is the sixth and last of Malachi's accusations: "'You have said harsh things against me,' says the Lord" (3:13 NIV). As he closes his book, he points out four different groups of people and what they said and did.

The complainers (3:13–15). These people were guilty of saying "harsh things" against the Lord. For one thing, they felt that serving the Lord was drudgery; it was "futile" to be His servants. The priests may have been the leaders in this complaining, but the common people were just as guilty. "We're not getting anything out of it!" was their grievance. "Things just keep getting worse."

I hear this complaint from some believers about their churches. "We're not getting anything out of it!" But a church is like a bank or a home: You don't get anything out of it unless you put something into it. We serve God because it's the right thing to do, not because we're rewarded for our service. (We shall be rewarded, but that's not our main motive.)

But they had a second complaint: The pagan peoples around them who didn't know the Lord were in better shape than the people of Judah! The wicked were prospering, while the godly were suffering. Of course, it would have been difficult for the Jews to prove that they were "godly," because they were guilty of disobeying the Lord. God would have blessed them if they had yielded themselves to Him, but they preferred to have their own way and then complain about what didn't happen.

It's a serious thing to serve the Lord, and we're commanded to "serve the Lord with gladness" (Ps. 100:2). It's a sad thing when servants of God drudge, merely doing a job because that's what they have to do or for what they get out of it. Philippians 2:1–12 is God's portrait of Christ, God's ideal Servant, and His example is the one that we should follow.

The believers (3:16–18). There was a group of true believers in this remnant, and they remained faithful to the Lord. They feared the Lord, which means they held Him in awe and worshipped Him as the Lord

Almighty. They met together, not to complain but to encourage and edify each other. They spoke about the Lord, and they weren't afraid for Him to hear what they were saying!

Their assembly probably wasn't a large one, and they may have thought that very little was happening because they met and worshipped, but God was paying attention and keeping a record of their words. Their neighbors may have laughed at them, but God was pleased with them. They weren't wasting their time because they were investing in eternity.

God claimed them as His own, and God promised to spare them in the future judgment when everybody would see that there is a difference between the righteous and the wicked and that this difference is important.

One of the sins of the priests was that they failed to make the distinction between the way of holiness and the way of sin. To them, one sacrifice was just as good as another, yet they were supposed to teach the people "the difference between the holy and the common, and show them how to distinguish between the unclean and the clean" (Ezek. 44:23 NIV).

Many of God's faithful servants become discouraged because the times are difficult, the crowds are small, and their work seems to be unappreciated. People who aren't really walking with the Lord seem to be getting more attention than are the faithful servants. But the day will come when God will reveal "his jewels" ("treasured possession," NIV; see Ex. 19:5; Deut. 7:6), and then the faithful will receive their reward. Every discouraged servant of God needs to read and ponder 1 Corinthians 4:1–5.

The evildoers (4:1–3). Once again, Malachi returns to the theme of the coming day of the Lord, when God will punish all evildoers. Sinners will be burned up the way fire eats up the stubble; they will become like ashes under the feet of the saints! But the true believers will see the dawning of a new day as the "Sun of righteousness" rises (Mal. 4:2; see also Luke 1:78–79). Then Jesus will reign as King of Kings and His people will frolic like calves let out of their stalls!

200 \ Be Amazed

The preachers (4:4–6). Malachi has been faithful as God's messenger, and he closes his book by reminding the people of two other faithful prophets, Moses and Elijah. The law of Moses was still God's rule of life for the Jews, and if they obeyed, God would bless them. Of course, believers today aren't under the law (Rom. 6:15; Gal. 5:1–4), but they still practice the righteousness of the law through the power of the indwelling Spirit of God (Rom. 8:1–4).

The promise in Malachi 4:5 was often discussed and debated by the Jewish rabbis, who asked, "Who is the Elijah whom the Lord will send?" The Jewish leaders interrogated John the Baptist about it (John 1:19–21); and Peter, James, and John asked Jesus about it (Matt. 17:10).

The prophet Elijah is mentioned at least thirty times in the New Testament, and ten of those references relate him to John the Baptist. But John the Baptist said plainly that he was no Elijah (John 1:21, 25). He did come in the "spirit and power" of Elijah and turn the hearts of fathers and children (Luke 1:16–17). Like Elijah, John was a courageous man, a man of prayer empowered by the Spirit, a man who lived alone in the wilderness, and a servant who turned many people back to the Lord, but he was not Elijah returned to earth.

However, for those who believed on Christ during His earthly ministry, John the Baptist performed the work of Elijah in their lives: He prepared them to meet the Lord. "And if you are willing to accept it, he is the Elijah who was to come" (Matt. 11:14 NIV). "Elijah is come already," said Jesus, "and they knew him not." The disciples understood Jesus to mean John the Baptist, who came in the spirit and power of Elijah (17:10–13).

But Malachi 4:5 promises that Elijah himself will come, and that his coming is related to the "day of the Lord" that will burn the wicked like stubble (v. 1). That's why Jesus said, "Elijah truly shall first come, and restore all things" (Matt. 17:11). Many students believe that Elijah is one of the two witnesses whose ministries are described in Revelation 11:3–12.

(They believe the other is Moses.) It's worth noting that both Moses and Elijah appeared with Jesus on the Mount of Transfiguration (Matt. 17:3), which explains why the three apostles asked about Elijah.

Inasmuch as "the great and terrible day of the Lord" did not occur in New Testament times, we have to believe that John the Baptist was not the promised Elijah, even though he ministered like Elijah. Therefore, this prophecy is yet to be fulfilled. It may well be that Elijah will return to earth as one of the two witnesses (Rev. 11:3–12), for the signs that these two men will perform remind us of the miracles of Elijah. After the ministry of the witnesses, the Lord will pour out His wrath upon the earth (v. 18; 16:1ff.) and the day of the Lord will burst upon the world in its fury.

It seems odd that the Old Testament Scriptures should end with the word *curse*. When we get near the end of the New Testament, we read, "And there shall be no more curse" (Rev. 22:3). All of creation is eagerly awaiting the return of the Savior, expecting Him to deliver creation from the bondage of sin (Rom. 8:18–23). We too should be expecting Him and, while we're waiting, witness of Him to others. For when the "Sun of righteousness" arises, it will mean either burning or blessing (Mal. 4:1–2): blessing to those who have trusted Him, burning to those who have rejected Him.

Nobody can afford to argue with God the way the Israelites did when they heard Malachi, because God will always have the last word.

For you, will that last word be salvation or judgment?

QUESTIONS FOR PERSONAL REFLECTION
OR GROUP DISCUSSION

1. How can we freely express our honest feelings to God without straying into the wrong of arguing with God? (Think about Habakkuk alongside Malachi.)

2. What does it mean that God grew weary of the Israelites' words?

3. Why weren't God's people experiencing His promises and blessings? Does this hold true for us today? Explain.

4. What was unique about the ministry of John the Baptist? How did John the Baptist prepare the way for Jesus?

5. How did the first coming of Christ answer the question "Where is the God of justice?" (2:17—3:1)? How will his second coming answer that question (3:2–5)?

6. How do you respond to the idea of Jesus Christ coming to purify His people with water and fire?

7. Who are "false swearers" (3:5)? Why are "false swearers" so dangerous? Whose words can you trust, and why?

8. How might we personally be oppressing the poor and needy?

9. What's the connection between these sins and the lack of appropriate fear of God (3:5)?

10. How is it robbery to fail to give generously to the work of God (3:6–12)?

11. What are the most important things you have learned from your study of the prophets in this book?

NOTES

HOSEA IN HIS TIME

1. Jeroboam I reigned from 931 to 910 BC, Jeroboam II from 793 to 753. The Jeroboam mentioned in Hosea 1:1 is Jeroboam II.

CHAPTER 1

1. See Isaiah 20; Jeremiah 27—28; Ezekiel 4:1–8; 5:1ff.; 12:1–16; 24:15ff.
2. When you study the commentaries, you discover a number of different views defended: (1) Gomer was a pure woman who later became a prostitute and bore Hosea three children; (2) Gomer was a pure woman who became a prostitute and bore Hosea a son, but also gave birth to a daughter and son who were not fathered by Hosea; (3) Gomer was a prostitute from the beginning and bore Hosea three children; (4) Gomer was a prostitute from the beginning and bore Hosea his own son, but also bore two children by another man; (5) Gomer was a prostitute who already had three children, but Hosea ultimately divorced her and married another woman who was an adulteress (3:1). It's easy to lose sight of the main message God wanted to get across: He loved His people and wanted them to return that love to Him. They were committing evil by worshipping idols, just like a woman who is unfaithful to her husband. They were not only sinning against God's law, but also sinning against God's love. As to the legitimacy of the children, the fact that 1:6 and 8 don't read "and bore him a daughter … a son" does not mean Hosea wasn't the father of these children. It seems natural to assume from the context that Hosea is the father. See Genesis 30:17–24 for a similar statement.

3. TLB reads, "Go and marry a girl who is a prostitute."

4. In Scripture, a change of names is often evidence of God's gracious
working in people's lives. Abram became Abraham, and Sarai was
renamed Sarah (Gen. 17). Simon became Peter (John 1:42), and Saul
of Tarsus became Paul (Paulus means "little").

5. Paul quoted Hosea 1:10 and 2:23 in Romans 9:25–26 to prove
that the salvation of the Gentiles was always a part of God's plan.
He applied "not my people" to the Gentiles as he did in Ephesians
2:11–22. In the early church, some of the more legalistic believers
thought that the Gentiles had to first become Jews before they could
be Christians (Acts 10—11; 15), but Paul defended the gospel of the
grace of God and proved that both Jews and Gentiles are saved by
grace through faith in Jesus Christ.

6. The Hebrew words referring to prostitutes and prostitution (KJV,
"whoredom," "harlotries") are used twenty-two times in Hosea's
prophecy (1:2, 2:2, 4–5; 3:3, 4:10–15, 18; 5:3–4; 6:10; 9:1). Words
connected with adultery are used six times (2:2; 3:1; 4:2, 13–14; 7:4).
God looked upon His covenant relationship with His people as a
marriage, and He saw their idolatry as marital unfaithfulness.

7. Hebrew law stated that a divorced woman could not return to her
former husband and marry him again (Deut. 24:1–4). God gave
unfaithful Israel a "divorce" in that He no longer shared His intimacy
and His mercies with her (Isa. 50:1; Jer. 3:1–5). One day He will take
her back and restore the broken relationship and heal their land (Isa.
54:4–8; 62:4).

8. Kyle M. Yates, *Preaching From the Prophets* (New York: Harper and
Brothers, 1942), 53.

CHAPTER 2

1. See Hosea 2:8, 20; 5:4; 8:2; 11:3; 13:4–5.

2. Compare Hosea 4:3 with Genesis 9:8–11 and Revelation 4:7–11, and you will see that God takes seriously His covenant with creation. He will one day judge those who destroy the earth (Rev. 11:18). The basis for ecology is not politics or comfort but the holy law of God. We are stewards of God's creation.

3. Jesus said to the Samaritan woman at Jacob's well, "You worship what you do not know; we know what we worship, for salvation is of the Jews" (John 4:22 NKJV). So much for the Samaritan religion or for any other man-made system of worship!

4. "A stick of wood" (Hos. 4:12 NIV; KJV, "their staff") may refer to the idol or to the heathen practice called rhabdomancy. (The Greek word *rhabdos* means "a rod.") The priest drew a circle on the ground and divided it into sections, with each section assigned a meaning. A rod was held in the center and then allowed to fall, and where it fell revealed the future.

5. Hosea 4:14 is a clear statement that God expects sexual purity and marital faithfulness from both men and women. In Israel, the men often got away with their sexual sins, while the women were punished. See Genesis 38 and John 8 for tragic examples of an unbiblical one-sided morality. Where was the man who assisted the woman in committing adultery? Wasn't he also supposed to be punished? See Leviticus 20:10 and Deuteronomy 22:22.

6. At one time, Gilgal was a sacred place where the Word of God was taught (2 Kings 2:1; 4:38). How quickly religious institutions can drift from their mooring and abandon the faith!

7. This may mean literal illegitimate children because of sexual promiscuity or children who were not a part of the covenant because of the sins of their parents during the pagan fertility rites. The sins of the fathers bring tragic consequences in the lives of the children.

8. Even Judah will be included in this discipline (Hos. 5:10). The Assyrians devastated Judah but were unable to capture Jerusalem, for

God delivered King Hezekiah and his people in a miraculous way. See Isaiah 36—37. The sin of Judah, according to Hosea, was that of seizing territory that wasn't rightfully theirs, like people who moved the boundary markers in order to increase their holding (Deut. 19:14; Isa. 5:8; Mic. 2:2).

9. The phrase "King Jareb" in Hosea 5:13 (KJV, NASB) is translated "the great king" in the NIV. The Hebrew word means "to contend, to strive." This could be a nickname for the king of Assyria, such as "King Contention." Israel and Judah turned to the king of Assyria for help and all he did was pick a fight!

10. This is made clear in 1 John 1, where the phrase "if we say" is repeated three times. See also King Saul's "religious lies" in 1 Samuel 15:10–35.

11. Since the Hebrew word translated "Adam" means "red earth," it's been suggested that verse 7 be translated, "They have treated the covenant like dirt." Adam also stands for mankind in general, so we might translate it, "Like mere humans, they have transgressed the covenant."

12. Dr. Leon Wood translated Hosea 8:5, "Your calf stinks!" *The Expositor's Bible Commentary*, Frank E. Gaebelein, gen. ed. (Grand Rapids: Zondervan, 1985), vol. 7, 201. J. B. Phillips isn't quite that blunt in his translation: "Samaria, I reject your calf with loathing!" *Four Prophets: A Translation Into Modern English* (New York: Macmillan, 1963), 41.

13. The adults sin and the children have to suffer: "Ephraim shall bring forth his children to the murderer" (9:13). When Hosea speaks in verse 14, he asks God to keep the women from having children so they won't be murdered. He is pleading for mercy for the innocent. See our Lord's words in Luke 23:29.

14. The vine as a symbol of the Jewish nation is also found in Deuteronomy 32:32; Psalm 80:8–11; Isaiah 5:1–7; and Jeremiah 2:21. The vine also pictures Christ and His church (John 15) and

the Gentile world system ripening for judgment in the last days (Rev. 14:17–20).

15. The references to Israel's past history—Baal-Peor (Hos. 9:10) and Gibeah (9:9; 10:9)—show that "the only thing we learn from history is that we don't learn from history." Both of these events brought the judgment of God on the nation, yet later generations turned a blind eye to this fact. The sins of the fathers are committed by their children—and grandchildren.

16. Any group that calls itself "the lost tribes of Israel" is suspect, for only God knows where all the tribes are. See Acts 26:7; James 1:1; and Revelation 7:1–8.

CHAPTER 3

1. The prophet Hosea was very familiar with Jewish history, not only what happened but also why it happened and how it related to the present and the future of his people. He refers to the exodus (2:15; 11:11;12:9, 13; 13:4), the events surrounding Jehu and Jezreel (1:4, 11; 2:22), Achan and the Valley of Achor (2:15), the wickedness of Gibeah (9:9; 10:9), Israel's sins at Baal-Peor (9:10), the destruction of the cities of the plain (11:8), and events in the life of Jacob (12:3–4, 12).

2. Hebrews 12:11–17 is the classic passage in Scripture on chastening. The Greek word *paideia* means "the rearing of a child," because the purpose of discipline is maturity. Sometimes God disciplines us to correct our disobedience, but He may also discipline us when we're obedient in order to equip us to serve Him better. David is an example of correcting discipline (2 Sam. 12; Ps. 32; 51), while Joseph is an example of perfecting discipline (Gen. 39—42; Ps. 105:16–22). Note that the context of Hebrews 12 is that of athletics, running the race (12:1–3). Athletes must experience the pain of discipline (dieting, exercising, competing) if they ever hope to excel. Nobody

ever mastered a sport simply by listening to a lecture or watching a video, as helpful as those encounters may be. At some point, the swimmer must dive into the water, the wrestler must hit the mat, and the runner must take his or her place on the track. Likewise, the children of God must experience the pain of discipline—correcting and perfecting—if they are to mature and become like Jesus Christ.

3. "Israel" is the new name God gave Jacob after struggling with him at Jabbok (Gen. 32:24–32), but scholars aren't agreed on its meaning. The generally accepted meaning is "prince with God" (i.e., a "God-controlled person"). Others suggest "he persists with God," which certainly fits the account; for Jacob wrestled with the angel of the Lord and didn't want to give in. Though Jacob made some mistakes and sometimes trusted his own ingenuity too much, he did persist with God and seek God's help, and God used him to build the nation of Israel. Some people have been too hard on Jacob, forgetting that believers in that day didn't have the advantages we have today. God has deigned to call Himself "the God of Jacob," and that's a very high compliment to a great man.

4. All of us are Jacobs at heart according to Jeremiah 17:9: "The heart is deceitful above all things, and desperately wicked: who can know it?" The Hebrew word translated "deceitful" is the root word for the name "Jacob." It means "to take by the heel, to supplant." The English word *supplant* comes from a Latin word that means to "to overthrow by tripping up." Jacob tripped up his brother and took his place when it came to both the family birthright and the blessing (Gen. 27:36). Of course, God had given both to Jacob before his birth (25:23), but instead of trusting God, Jacob used his own devices to get what he wanted. Faith is living without scheming.

5. These two names suggest the two aspects of our Lord's life and ministry, a Man of Sorrows and the resurrected Son exalted to the Father's right hand.

6. When New Testament writers quoted Old Testament statements, the Holy Spirit directing them had every right to adapt those passages as He wished, since the Spirit is the author of Scripture. Surely God sees much more in His Word than we do! For example, Hosea 11:1 refers to Israel's exodus from Egypt, but Matthew used it to point to Christ's coming out of Egypt when a child (Matt. 2:11–15).

7. Biblical images must be studied carefully and identified accurately, for the same image may be used with different meanings in different contexts. The dew is a case in point. In Hosea 6:4, it represents the fleeting religious devotion of the hypocrites, while in 13:3, it symbolizes the transiency of the people who think they're so secure. Both Jesus and Satan are represented by the lion (Rev. 5:5; 1 Peter 5:8).

JOEL IN HIS TIME

1. The term *day of the Lord* is used to describe the fall of Israel in 722 BC (Amos 5), the fall of Judah in 586 BC (Ezek. 13:5), and the battle of Carchemish in 605 BC (Jer. 46:10). Each of these local calamities was a precursor of the worldwide judgment that is promised by the prophets and also by our Lord (Matt. 24; Mark 13).

OUTLINE OF THE BOOK OF JOEL

1. The "imminent" day of the Lord refers to the future invasion of Judah by the Assyrians, when the land would be devastated and Jerusalem surrounded by armies. (See Isa. 36—37; 2 Kings 18—19; and 2 Chron. 32.) This occurred during the reign of King Hezekiah (715–686 BC). Jerusalem was miraculously delivered from Assyria by the angel of the Lord who killed 185,000 Assyrian soldiers in one night. However, not every Old Testament student sees a distinction between I and II. Some see II as an amplification of I. Regardless of how you outline the book, the message remains the same: Each

national calamity reminds us that the "day of the Lord" is coming and we must be prepared.

CHAPTER 4

1. In the KJV, the Hebrew word is translated "old men" in 1:2 and 2:28, and "elders" in 1:14 and 2:16. The NIV uses "elders" everywhere except 2:28, where the contrast between "young men" and "old men" is quite obvious. It's possible that the "old men" were indeed the official elders of the land.

2. The phrase "your God" is used eight times in this book to remind the people of their personal relationship to Jehovah and their accountability to Him (1:13–14; 2:13–14, 23, 26–27; 3:17).

3. "Almighty" is a translation of the Hebrew word *Shaddai*, which is related to the Hebrew word for "breast." He is the all-sufficient One, the bountiful One, the God who can do anything. The name is found forty-eight times in the Old Testament, thirty-one of them in the book of Job, where the greatness of God is one of the major themes. "Almighty" is used eight times in the book of Revelation.

4. Why should Joel call the people to repent in order to avoid an invasion that would take place a century later? Because they didn't know when the invasion would come, and their brokenness before God was the means of postponing it. We look back and see that Isaiah 36—37 fulfilled what Joel wrote, but the people of Judah were looking ahead into an unknown future. It's always right to repent and submit to the will of God. That's the best way to secure the future.

5. The repeated use of the word *like* in 2:4–7 indicates that Joel is using a simile and not describing the actual army. The locusts looked and acted like an army, and the invading Assyrian army would be like them: numerous, ruthless, destructive, and invincible. When you

get to 2:8–11, you are reading about real soldiers in a real battle: for locusts don't worry about swords.

6. God is said to "repent" when from man's point of view He changes His attitude and turns away His wrath. The word "relent" might be a better choice.

7. Charles H. Spurgeon, *Metropolitan Tabernacle Pulpit* (Pasadena, TX: Pilgrim Publications, 1977), vol. 35, 217.

8. There may be a hint here that some of the people were involved in idolatry and needed to turn from heathen vanities and worship only the Lord (Ex. 20:1–6).

CHAPTER 5

1. Note that the phrase "a thousand years" is used six times in Revelation 20:1–7. The Latin word for "thousand years" is *millennium*; it is used to describe the kingdom Jesus Christ will establish on earth in fulfillment of the Old Testament promises to Israel. However, some students prefer to "spiritualize" these promises and apply them to the church today, and these people are called amillennialists, meaning "no millennium." Premillennialists are Christians who believe Jesus will return before the kingdom is established, for how can you have a kingdom without the King? There was a time when a postmillennial interpretation was popular: The church would "change the world" and "bring in the kingdom," and then Jesus would return to reign. The wars and atrocities of this past century and the spread of apostasy in the church have pretty well done away with this optimistic outlook.

2. Some say that the darkening of the sun from noon until three o'clock (Matt. 27:45) and the local earthquake (vv. 51–54) after Jesus' crucifixion fulfilled Joel's promise, but Matthew doesn't say so. Invariably, when something happened that fulfilled Scripture, Matthew calls it to our attention (26:24, 56; 27:9, 35). At least twelve

times in his gospel, Matthew uses the word *fulfilled* to point to an Old Testament messianic prophecy, but he doesn't include Joel 2:28–32.

3. In Scripture, you sometimes find "near" and "distant" fulfillments of God's promises. The "near" fulfillment is partial, while the "distant" fulfillment is complete. In 2 Samuel 7, God promised to build David a house. The near fulfillment was the Davidic dynasty that ruled until Judah was exiled to Babylon. The distant fulfillment is found in Jesus Christ, the Son of David, whose reign shall never end (Luke 1:32–33).

4. To make the "valley of decision" a place where lost sinners decide to follow Christ is to twist the Scripture. It is God who makes the decision, and His decision (decree) is to judge and not save. The nations have had their opportunity; now it is too late.

5. Pretribulationists believe that the church will be taken to heaven (raptured) before the day of the Lord breaks upon the world (1 Thess. 1:10; 5:9–10). This event is described in 1 Thessalonians 4:13–18. The saints will then return to the earth with Jesus when He returns in glory to defeat His enemies and establish His kingdom (Rev. 19:11ff.; 2 Thess. 2). Prophetic students differ as to the details of the end-times scenario, but they agree that the world will grow hostile against God, the people of God will suffer persecution, and the Lord will return to conquer His enemies and rescue His people. This is what we are asking when we pray, "Thy kingdom come."

CHAPTER 6

1. The KJV translates the Hebrew connective "now," while the NIV and NASB ignore it completely.

2. Jonah's hometown of Gath Hepher was on the border of Zebulun, one of the northernmost tribes, and therefore extremely vulnerable to the attacks of invaders. Perhaps he had seen what the Assyrians could do.

3. Tarshish was probably in Spain, over one thousand miles west of Joppa. Jonah was supposed to travel east to Nineveh. The Jews weren't seafarers, but Jonah forgot his prejudices and fears in his attempt to escape doing God's will.

4. It was at Joppa that Peter got his divine call to go to the Gentiles with the message of the gospel (Acts 10). Though he protested somewhat at first, unlike Jonah, he obeyed God's call and opened the door of faith to the Gentiles. What a privilege!

5. One exception is when the fall of the Jews brought salvation to the Gentiles (Rom. 11:11ff.). Israel was out of God's will when they rejected Christ and opposed the gospel, but this opened the door of salvation to the Gentiles.

6. The word translated "regard" means "to look upon with knowledge and approval." It isn't only knowing that we've sinned that hinders prayer, but holding on to that sin, approving of it, and protecting it. (See 1 John 1:5–10.)

7. It appears that the sailors gave Jonah a nickname: "he who is responsible for causing all this trouble" (Jonah 1:8 NIV). Since the lot had already fallen on Jonah, the crew didn't need to ask him who was to blame. He was to blame, and they knew it; and that's why they gave him that embarrassing nickname. The KJV, NASB, and NIV all make the nickname into an unnecessary question.

8. The fact that Jonah wanted to die even after Nineveh was delivered (4:8–9) indicates that his heart was still bitter and unyielding with reference to God's will. A surrendered servant will say, "Not my will but Thy will be done."

9. Jonah 1:17 in the English versions is Jonah 2:1 in the Hebrew text.

10. Some expositors believe that Jonah actually died and was resurrected, and base their interpretation on statements in his prayer like "From the depths of the grave [sheol—the realm of the dead] I called for

help" (2:2 NIV) and "But you brought my life up from the pit" (v. 6 NIV). But Jonah's prayer is composed of quotations from at least fifteen different psalms, and while some of these psalms describe near-death experiences, none describes a resurrection miracle. The reference to sheol in verse 2 comes from Psalm 30:3 (and see 16:10 and 18:4–6), and the reference to "the pit" comes from 49:15, both of which were written by David. If these two psalms describe Jonah's resurrection, then they must also describe David's resurrection, but we have no evidence that David ever died and was raised to life. Instead, these psalms describe frightening experiences when God delivered His servants from the very gates of death. That seems to be what Jonah is describing as he quotes them in his prayer. Furthermore, if Jonah died and was resurrected, he could not be an accurate type of Christ (Matt. 12:39; 16:4; Luke 11:29); for types picture the antitype but don't duplicate it, for the antitype is always greater. It's a dangerous thing to build an interpretation on the poetic language of Scripture when we don't have a clear New Testament interpretation to lean on.

11. "There is a sin unto death" (1 John 5:17). "The Lord shall judge his people. It is a fearful thing to fall into the hands of the living God" (Heb. 10:30–31). Professed believers who play with sin and trifle with God's loving discipline are asking for trouble. Better that we should die than that we should resist His will and bring disgrace to the name of Christ.

CHAPTER 7

1. Charles H. Spurgeon, *Metropolitan Tabernacle Pulpit* (Pasadena, TX: Pilgrim Publication, 1977), vol. 42, 73.

2. "Great" is one of the key words in the book of Jonah. Besides a "great city," the book mentions a great wind and tempest (1:4, 12); great fear (vv. 10, 16); a great fish (v. 17); great people, probably nobles (3:5, 7); and Jonah's great displeasure and great gladness (4:1–6).

3. Some date Nineveh's founding as early as 4500 BC.

4. The early church faced this problem when Peter took the gospel to the Gentiles (Acts 10—11; 15). According to Jewish theology, Gentiles had to become Jews (proselytes) before they could become Christians, but Cornelius and his family and friends were saved simply by believing on Jesus Christ. When Peter said "whoever believes in Him will receive remission of sins" (v. 43 NKJV), the people present believed the promise, trusted Christ, and the Holy Spirit came upon them. Peter never got to finish his sermon (10:43–48). The legalistic Jews in the Jerusalem church argued later that Gentiles could not be saved apart from obeying the law of Moses, and Paul had to debate with them to protect the truth of the gospel (Acts 15; Gal. 1). Jonah would have sided with the legalists.

5. Both Moses (Num. 11) and Elijah (1 Kings 19) became so discouraged that they made the same request. We lose our perspective when we focus on ourselves and fail to look by faith to the Lord (Heb. 12:1–2).

6. The phrase in 4:11 "and also much cattle" reminds us of God's concern for animal life. God preserves both man and beast (Ps. 36:6), and the animals look to God for their provision (104:10–30). God has made a covenant with creation (Gen. 9:1–17); and even in the law of Moses, He shows concern for His creation (Deut. 22:6–7; Lev. 22:26–28). An understanding of God is the basis for a true ecology.

7. Alexander Whyte, *Bible Characters from the Old and New Testaments* (Grand Rapids, MI: Kregel Publications, 1990), 387.

8. Charles H. Spurgeon, 84.

CHAPTER 8

1. Nineveh was destroyed by the Medes and Babylonians in 612 BC, but the empire didn't collapse immediately. Remnants of the army

and of political leadership struggled on until they were overpowered in 609 at the battle of Haran. But when Nineveh fell, it was the death knell for the empire.

2. Lebanon on the north, Carmel on the east, and Bashan on the west were known for their fruitfulness. See Isaiah 2:13; 33:9; and 35:2.

3. Isaiah 10:5–18 explains that Assyria was God's tool ("the rod of My anger" NKJV) to chasten Judah because of her idolatry, but the Assyrians had gone too far and been too ruthless. In his pride, the king of Assyria had boasted of his past victories, so the Lord announced that He would humble him. This God did when His angel destroyed 185,000 Assyrian soldiers in one night (37:36–38; see 10:16).

4. Nahum 1:15 in our English versions is 2:1 in the Hebrew text. What a contrast between the announcement of peace in 1:15 and the declaration of war in 2:1!

5. "Jacob" probably refers to Judah, the southern kingdom, and Israel refers to the northern kingdom that was dispersed by Assyria in 722–721 BC. Since this promise has not been fulfilled, its fulfillment awaits the return of Christ when He will establish His kingdom and restore the splendor of the Jewish nation.

6. This image is not meant to demean women in any way, whether civilians or in the armed forces, or to suggest that women lack strength and courage. The biblical examples of Rahab, Deborah, Jael, Ruth, and Esther prove that Scripture can magnify the courage and service of dedicated women. However, we must keep in mind that the ancient world was a masculine society; women were kept secluded and certainly wouldn't have been expected to participate in battles. Phrases like "weak as a woman" were current; both Isaiah (19:16) and Jeremiah (50:37; 51:30) used them.

OUTLINE OF THE BOOK OF HABAKKUK

1. The four statements in italics are the three assurances God gave to
   Habakkuk in the midst of the "woes." They remind us that, no matter
   how difficult life may become, God's promises can be trusted (v. 4),
   His glory will one day prevail (v. 14), and He is on His holy throne in
   complete control of people and events (v. 20). When Habakkuk realized this, he broke out into singing (chap. 3).

CHAPTER 9

1. Paul quoted verse 5 at the close of his message in the synagogue in
   Antioch of Pisidia (Acts 13:41; and see also Isa. 29:14). It was a warning to the people not to treat the gospel lightly and thereby reject it.
   The original statement to Habakkuk referred to the coming of the
   Babylonians, but Paul applied it to the saving work of Jesus Christ
   and the offer of the gospel. Both were incredible works of God.
2. What Habakkuk suffered in a small way, Job suffered in a great
   way, and God's answer to Job's many questions was simply to reveal
   Himself to Job. We don't live on explanations, we live on promises,
   and the promises of God are based on the character of God. The
   turning point in Job's experience came when he put his hand on his
   mouth, stopped arguing with the Lord, and began to worship the
   Lord (Job 40:1–5; 42:1–6). Habakkuk had a similar experience.
   There's nothing like a fresh view of the glory of God to give you
   strength for the journey!
3. Jeremiah would fill in the details and explain that the people would be
   in exile for seventy years. After that, a remnant would return to Judah,
   rebuild the temple, and establish the nation. See Jeremiah 25 and 29.
4. His question "Why are you silent?" (v. 13 NIV) has been asked by
   both saints and sinners for centuries. Of course, God is not silent,
   because He speaks through His Word to those who have ears to

hear. He spoke the loudest at Calvary when His beloved Son died on the cross; for the atonement is God's final and complete answer to the sins of the world. Because of the cross, God is both "just and the justifier" (Rom. 3:26). He has both upheld His holy law and manifested His loving heart. Sin has been judged and the way has been opened for sinners to become the children of God. Nobody can complain about such a wise and loving answer!

CHAPTER 10

1. Commentators and translators don't agree on what "that he may run that readeth it" (v. 2) really means. The NIV translates it "so that a herald may run with it" and the NASB says "[so] that the one who reads it may run." The NRSV translates it "so that a runner may read it," and F. F. Bruce puts it "so that one who reads it may read with ease" (*An Exegetical and Expository Commentary on the Minor Prophets,* edited by Thomas E. McComiskey [Baker Book House, 1993], vol. 2, 858). Bruce explains the phrase to mean "not that the person who reads it will start running, but rather that the reader will be able to take it in at a glance, so large and legible is the writing; the eye will run over the text with ease." That seems to be what the Lord said to Habakkuk.

2. The KJV translation of 2:6b is a bit puzzling: "And to him that ladeth himself with thick clay!" The image seems to be that of a creditor giving a pledge to the banker (a clay tablet) and promising to pay his debt at a specific time. Habakkuk wrote, "The predator (Babylon) is really a creditor and his victims will one day rise up to collect what is due. It will be payday!" F. F. Bruce translates verse 6b: "Woe to him who multiplies what is not his own—but for how long? And loads himself with pledges" (F. F. Bruce, 864).

3. Jesus used the image of the stones crying out when He cleansed the temple and the children sang His praises (Luke 19:40). If people don't

praise God, inanimate nature will do it! The idea of stones bearing witness goes back to Joshua 24:27.

4. Isaiah promised that "the earth shall be full of the knowledge of the Lord" (11:9), a phrase that relates to Numbers 14:21. When the seraphim before God's throne look upon the earth, they see it full of God's glory (Isa. 6:3), though it may not look glorious from our perspective. When we pray "Thy kingdom come," we are praying for Habakkuk 2:14 to be fulfilled. "Let the whole earth be filled with his glory" (Ps. 72:19).

5. Some see in this the picture of the conqueror giving the conquered rulers a cup of poison to drink. However, the emphasis seems to be on disgrace rather than death.

CHAPTER 11

1. We don't know what the Hebrew word *Shigionoth* means. Some scholars trace it to a root that means "to reel to and fro," so perhaps *Shigionoth* was a musical term that told the people how the psalm was to be sung. Three times in the psalm you find "Selah" (vv. 3, 9, 13), another Hebrew word whose meaning and significance are still a mystery. Some say it marks a pause in the psalm for the reader (or singer and listeners) to ponder what was said.

2. The phrase "in the midst of the years" (3:2) probably refers to the period between Habakkuk's time and "the appointed time" when the vision would be fulfilled (2:3). Throughout the centuries, God's people have prayed for quickening power so that God's great work will prosper. While the word *revival* as we think of it wasn't in Habakkuk's mind, the concept is there. See Psalms 44 and 85.

3. Writing about his experience at the Transfiguration (2 Peter 1:15–21), the apostle Peter points out that the written Word is superior to glorious experiences. Only a few people can have rapturous experiences, but any believer can ponder them in the Word with the Spirit's help.

The people who had these great experiences have died, but the Word lives on. The memories of experiences will fade, but the Word remains the same. We now have a completed Bible, so the New Testament sheds light on the experiences of people like Moses, David, and the prophets; and we can see things that perhaps they didn't see. So, instead of saying, "I wish I could have that kind of experience," we should be asking, "Lord, what do You want to teach me from this experience?"

4. These mighty revelations of God in history are called "theophanies," from two Greek words meaning "an appearance of a god." For other examples, see Psalms 18; 68; and 77; and Exodus 15 and 19; and Deuteronomy 33.

5. The KJV has "measured" while the NIV has "shook" (v. 6). It all depends on what root you select, the Hebrew or the Arabic. Perhaps both ideas are included.

6. For other poetic descriptions of Israel's history, see Psalms 44; 68; 74; 78; 80; 83; 89; 105–106; 135; and 136.

7. William Cowper's hymn "God Moves in a Mysterious Way" is based partly on this hymn in Habakkuk 3.

8. G. Campbell Morgan, *The Westminster Pulpit* (London: Pickering and Inglis, 1970), vol. 6, 153.

OUTLINE OF THE BOOK OF MALACHI

1. Note that the book of Malachi is written as a dialogue between God and the people: God accused and they answer to defend themselves. See 1:2, 6–7, 12–13; 2:14, 17; 3:7–8, 13–14. Note also Malachi's emphasis on the name of God (1:6, 11, 14; 2:2, 5; 3:16; 4:2) and his reminder that God wants His name to be known by the Gentiles (1:11; 3:12).

CHAPTER 12

1. Eugene Peterson, *Run with the Horses* (Downers Grove, IL: InterVarsity Press, 1983), 69.

2. The word *shema* is Hebrew for "hear," the first word in the prayer.

3. In His sovereign grace, God often rearranged the birth order of children. Abel was older than Seth, but God chose Seth (Gen. 4:25–26). Ishmael was Abraham's firstborn son, but God bypassed him for Isaac (17:15–22). Manasseh was Joseph's firstborn, but God gave the blessing to Ephraim (48:13–22). This may be a reminder to us that in our first birth we are undone and without blessing, but because of the new birth, the second birth, we are "blessed with all spiritual blessings" in Christ (Eph. 1:3).

4. Zechariah 2:12 is the only place in Scripture where Palestine is called "the holy land." Malachi 3:12 calls it "a delightful land" (NIV); and it is also called a "Beautiful Land" (Dan. 11:41 NIV; "glorious"), "the Lord's land" (Hos. 9:3), and "the pleasant land" (Zech. 7:14).

5. For a full discussion of the verse, see *The Encyclopedia of Bible Difficulties* by Gleason L. Archer (Grand Rapids: Zondervan, 1982), 305–306.

6. Some people are surprised that a God of love could hate anything, but see Proverbs 6:16–19, as well as Psalms 5:5 and 11:5; Amos 5:21; Zechariah 8:17; and Revelation 2:6 and 15. "Ye who love the Lord, hate evil!" (Ps. 97:10) and see 139:21–22.

7. If God hates divorce, then why did He allow it? God permitted the Jews to divorce their wives if the wives were given a certificate that protected their reputation so they could be married again. However, they could not return to their first husband (Deut. 24:1–4). Jesus made it clear that the permission of divorce was a concession and not a commandment (Matt. 19:1–12), but God, the Author of marriage, can do it. Good and godly people disagree on the interpretation and application of the New Testament teachings concerning divorce and remarriage, and few if any are consistent in the way they handle the matter. It would appear that sexual sin would be grounds for divorce, and so would desertion (1 Cor. 7:12–16).

8. Deuteronomy 22:30 reads literally, "A man should not marry his father's wife; he must not uncover the corner of his father's garment."

CHAPTER 13

1. Keep in mind that the old covenant was not ended by the birth of Jesus in the manger but by the death of Jesus on the cross. John's ministry took place at the close of the old dispensation, so strictly speaking, he was an Old Testament prophet.

2. Some of the old editions of the Bible made this same mistake in their chapter headings. If the chapter was about blessing, the caption read "God's blessing on the church," but if it was about judgment the heading said, "God's judgment on the Jews." Yet the Bible tells us that "judgment must begin at the house of God" (1 Peter 4:17).

3. The offering mentioned in 1 Corinthians 16:1–3 was not a regular weekly offering received at a meeting of God's people. It was a special "relief offering" Paul was receiving from the Gentile believers to give aid to the Jewish Christians in Jerusalem.

4. Multitudes of people have testified to the blessing of regular systematic proportionate giving. However, we must remember that even after we've given generously to the Lord, what remains is still His, for we are stewards of everything He gives us. Giving a tithe doesn't mean we have the right to use the remaining 90 percent for ourselves.